Neighbor and Kin

Kenneth M. Sanchagrin
P.O. Box 507
Mars Hill, N.C. 28754

Neighbor
and
Kin

Life in a Tennessee Ridge Community

BY ELMORA MESSER MATTHEWS

Vanderbilt ∿ University Press: 1965

Dedicated to those country churches that have not died easily and to the kinship communities that have loved and lost them.

Foreword

THIS BOOK makes, in my opinion, three important contributions to sociology: the description of a community wherein conflict is an essential social condition for stability and continuity, the analysis of the social effects of bilateral kindreds under conditions where marriage choice is restricted to members of a closed community adds to our understanding of family structure, and the challenge to the general theory of stratification in sociology which claims that no community can exist without stratification. This community is a clear exception to that rule.

The author discovered about sixty families in which intermarriage had taken place since 1786. Facts were ascertained from them, on relations between families, relations between kindred, and relations within the community. As data accumulated from informants, however, it became apparent that some thirty of these families lived a co-operative, peaceful life, while the other thirty shot each other regularly. A search of local records of births and deaths at the County Court and in local newspapers confirmed beyond any doubt that violence within and between persons of the same kindred had existed for more than a century. This sort of endemic violence should lead to a questioning of the basic postulates of both consensus and conflict theories in sociology. Here we have a case wherein murder, accident, suicide, and other types of sudden death occur within a community that is obviously in a state of equilibrium.

An analogous case might be our national concern about

300 deaths a week in a couple of battles in Vietnam but little concern at all about 500 deaths on the roads during a national holiday that lasts only three days. The quotation in the book, " 'sometimes, and fur as long as anyone can remember, there'll be a full-scale war, people get slaughtered, and then the next day you'd never know what happened,' " [1] indicates that violence and death are a normal and expected category of event.

It is important to be clear that the book is *not* concerned with the feud between family lineages. Feuding occurs in Tennessee and elsewhere in the world, but it is a different form of social behavior from the violence here described. The analysis focuses on endemic violence in a part of a community. Under such names as "pervasive factionalism," similar social behavior has been described as an aspect of communities in India, in South America, and in other states in the United States.

The explanation of violence in one part of the community must rest on something that is an aspect of the community rather than an aspect of the family, for these families intermarry freely within the boundaries of the whole community. The feud rests on behavior learned in the family: its continuity from generation to generation and the specificity of its targets demonstrate that point. Endemic violence, with its sporadic and unpredictable outbreaks, must rest on a different set of factors. The search for these is one brilliant and original contribution made by this research.

To solve the problem of how a community may use violence as a factor in maintaining stable relations between its members over several generations, the book uses concepts from anthropology and sociology. The principal concepts are those of community and family. Although most sociologists accept communities and families as universal groups found in every society, there is little agreement about how these terms should

1. P. 138.

be conceived. To an anthropologist, a community "contains within it persons and roles and statuses, or the transmitted and learned awareness of them, for every kind and office of mankind that the culture knows: husband, artisan, miser, mother, priest, criminal, aristocrat, heretic, etc. The list is different for every human culture." [2] A sociologist would probably prefer to call this a subcultural group, yet the distinguishing marks of the community used by the sociologist are similar. "A community is a territorially-organized system co-extensive with a settlement pattern in which (1) an effective communication network operates, (2) people share common facilities and services distributed within this settlement pattern and (3) develop a psychological identification with the 'locality-symbol' (the name)." [3]

A community, then, should have a distinguishing set of beliefs or values (a culture); a distinctive set of positions and roles, one aspect of which is a network of communication; a territory in which to operate; and, as a social organization, the power to last longer than one lifetime. To make certain of this, it has to include provisions for sexual recruitment of new members and for training them in the beliefs and values of the culture. Locality, social interaction, and the persistence and distinctiveness of a cultural heritage are the common elements of the term "community." The difficulty is not in collecting definitions: they exist by the hundred. Analytical problems arise when we ask how this social group differs from a society or, more exactly, at what points and along what dimensions communities and societies interact. This set of analytical problems, however, is not our present concern. The social group in this book is a community, as that word is understood by both anthropologists and sociologists. The separateness, the long persistence of this kinship culture, and

2. C. M. Arensberg and S. T. Kimball, *Culture and Community* (New York: Harcourt-Brace, 1965), p. 21.

3. I. T. Sanders, *The Community* (New York: Ronald Press, 1958), p. 189.

the occupancy of a distinct territory are adequately documented in the text that follows.

Relations between families and communities, like the relations between communities and societies, are, as yet, not well understood. Formerly, many believed that the family was the building block out of which more complex groups such as societies were built. Social organization, however, rests as a minimum on the presence of a three-generational structure. Given two sexes and three generations, we have a sufficient time span and an adequate complement of positions to presuppose the coexistence of community and family. The law of incest, which appears to be a universal social norm, makes at least two families essential for the continuity of the social system. An older, postbreeding generation appears to be essential for cultural continuity, as distinct from biological continuity.

The family is the unit that transmits cultural beliefs to neonates: it never creates these beliefs anew each generation. With appropriate socialization, adolescents move into positions in the community. The rules of inheritance of family names and of family possessions, the production of material resources such as food or housing, the availability of age mates to choose among at the point of marriage, and the sense of identity both as family member and as a social being—all depend on the existence of social structures wider than the immediate domestic group. The complementary interpenetration of community and family structures rather than their existence as separate entities is the essential base for sociological or anthropological analysis.

To unravel complex social interrelations at the level of community-family and to use this analysis to explain certain important facets of human behavior calls for intellectual skill —and a certain amount of luck. Since social scientists cannot experiment, they are dependent upon the discovery of cases which exemplify certain experimental conditions. The community-family social system of this study is closed against outsiders: certain specialists such as the auctioneer, the preacher, or the teacher provide sporadic services. Their lack of residence allows the community to use them for its purposes, rather than to be drawn into the ambience of other types of social organization. The closure is made effective through the operation of endogamy.

The second contribution mentioned above, the contribution to family sociology, becomes possible because this population is American. They have the same feelings and attitudes, the same sense of rights and obligations, toward their relatives that we have. They count their relatives as we do: father, mother, grandfather, grandmother, cousin, uncle, aunt, niece, and nephew. That is to say, while the family bears the name of the father, relatives are not named differently on the father's nor on the mother's side, so that a cousin is a cousin and an uncle is an uncle irrespective of whether the relative belongs to the mother's or the father's side of the family unit. This bilateral system-of-descent terminology has certain consequences for both family and community structures, one of which is a tendency for the newly married to set up a home of their own, since no family rules are in existence to tell them to prefer to live with the husband's or the wife's people after marriage. Although more than one-third of all the societies in the world have bilateral descent systems, and these range from the Eskimo, to the Javanese, to the Irish, and to the population of the United States, we know little about the operation of the rules of descent in them. All, however, seem to favor a domestic unit of husband-wife and their children, a unit known as the nuclear family. Most sociologists hold that the nuclear family is either a product of, or peculiarly suited to, urban industrial civilization. The fact that it is widespread in societies at many different technical levels has not yet been fully assimilated.

Intermarriage within a bilateral set of families small enough to allow us to see the social effects of this particular descent system in our own culture offers a special opportunity to sociologists. The effectiveness of a double set of relatedness among those who marry in preserving the closed community is evident in the text. The desirability of a double bond between spouses is fully explained and is a real contribution. Most modern bilateral communities are open rather than closed, and for this reason the sociological consequences of bilaterality are difficult to trace. Added to this is the looseness introduced into the system by free choice of individuals in the decision to marry. An interesting new proposition states the limits of choice in such a way that the whole population of the United States may be considered the group within which a marriage choice is made: this is the concept of permanent availability for marriage between any two adults of the United States regardless of whether they are already married.[4] In the closed community of this study this type of analysis cannot arise. The juxtaposition of bilateral descent and endogamy, however, gives a special importance to this research.

A third contribution to our basic understanding of society is the discovery of a community without stratification. Specialization of work by age and sex occurs, but stratification as it is known in other parts of the United States seems to be absent. Achievement as a normative base for an individual career is not only absent, it would be positively disruptive. Success is defined not by excelling nor by doing better than others but by equalizing life chances so that everyone has the same access to those resources available to the community: food and shelter, land and implements, prestige and status. The conclusion is that violence occurs when families sharing a culture that is truly egalitarian attempt to secure for their lineal descendants resources in land, goods, women, or services that are believed to be in excess of those available to others.

A basic proposition in the theory of stratification is that all societies distribute the "goods" they produce differentially:

4. Bernard Farber, *Family: Organization and Interaction* (San Francisco: Chandler, 1964).

some positions are entitled to a larger share than others, and this is believed to be right and is supported by reference to certain legal and moral norms. Otherwise the structure of the society or community as a set of morals and motives that serve as a guide for individuals would be in a perpetual state of turmoil as the "have-nots" struggled to get a larger share from the "haves." Although such struggles occur in complex communities, the right of some to greater rewards than others is believed to be proper and is legal. This is true in both communistic and capitalistic societies. An absence of status distinctions marks an absence of unequal shares. Equality of opportunity to participate in the competition for positions that carry status privileges is not incompatible with their perpetuation. In complex communities "equality" usually means "equality of opportunity" in this sense.

An egalitarian culture, such as that described in this book, attempts to secure equal shares for every member. The sociological consequences of this and the dynamics by which the system is maintained are adequately documented. I want here to accept this as an established fact and to point to its implications for the theory of stratification. Without differential distribution of resources, states the theory, individuals will be neither trained nor motivated to occupy positions of leadership that call for postponement of gratification. In the culture described in this book close relations between age-mates, double-bonded kinsfolk, and lack of individuals who fill leader roles are interconnected. In work-teams, no one is clearly leader: collective responsibility for work assignment is the rule to an extent that to speak of individual or family farming enterprises would be to violate the facts. The area is best described as a closed corporate community; yet it is not a single collective farming enterprise, for each family owns its land and manages the sale of its crops. Borrowing, sharing, swapping out, helping by gifts those who are in need, all operate as mechanisms to redistribute scarce goods and services so that everyone has substantially the same. This is no primitive, preindustrial, preliterate, isolated, non-American culture: these people live with bathrooms, electricity, television, refrigerators, and full larders, as do other Americans. Yet they operate within a truly egalitarian culture and their community has shown great powers of survival.

Without a recognizable system of stratification, this should not have been possible. The fact that it can happen calls for a revision of our basic definition of stratification. This revision must, as a minimum, recognize that under some social structures tendencies toward differential rewards may be canceled out. An alternative formulation might consider that stratification as an element in community structure can only arise when family inheritance patterns become differentiated from those of community members in general. As the text says, "given consensus of goals only on a community level plus integration on the basis of mechanical solidarity . . . a society has adaptation without stratification."[5]

Finally, I should like to pay my personal tribute to Elmora Matthews. She began to write another descriptive study of a rural community, but her fine analytical mind led her to question and re-question her assumptions. Turning to the general stock of propositions available to sociologists, she used the work of such theorists as Talcott Parsons and R. K. Merton. Her original theoretical combination of the concepts bilateral kindred, closed corporate peasant community, egalitarian life chances, and congruence in normative structures of family and community give us an explanation of endemic violence that is both powerful and elegant. Through all of this two-year long intellectual struggle she worked with tremendous industry and diligence. Unlike the folk she describes, this is a clear case of deferred gratification. My wish now is that she should reap all the rewards our system of stratification provides.

JOHN MOGEY

Boston University
December 1965

5. *Ibid.*, p. 133.

Preface

PROFESSOR MOGEY has contributed more to this book than its foreword. He has encouraged the research and writing throughout. He has given effective help with tools and structural insights. My three sons and husband have generously shared valuable information and have collected male questionnaires.

I hope I shall be able to repay the four men in my family. It will be more difficult to repay John Mogey. And most remote is the possibility that I can discharge my debt to those Tennessee valley families whose way of life I deeply respect and whom I have loved as friends.

I have used fictitious names to protect specific places and people and, in a few cases, have disguised events and individuals with modal characteristics. The more general settings are accurately named to add meaning and interest.

Though these pages contain concrete and personal accounts, it is my hope that many readers will substitute family and community names of their own.

ELMORA MESSER MATTHEWS

Department of Sociology
University of Texas
April 1965

Contents

PART III. EVALUATION

List of Tables

Illustrations

Introduction of the So-Sos

THIS BOOK is about a familiar type of American community—"where everybody's kin to everybody else." The kinship community is as old as our nation. Yet its structure is as puzzling to us as the genealogical charts of our own bilateral kinship networks.

Neighbor and kin in our community often refer to themselves and to their respected fellow residents as ordinary folks or as So-Sos. A So-So is one who is neither higher nor lower than those around him, neither richer nor poorer, neither more nor less educated, neither more saintly nor more devilish. When asked how he is, he usually describes his condition as "passable," "fair-to-middling," "tolerable," or "so-so."

The significant thing about the So-So is that he works at being ordinary. He seeks the medium rank, the moderate state. That is, he seeks those activities and qualities which do not set him apart in any way from his neighbors. The So-Sos have thus achieved a remarkably equal distribution of goods and services within a remarkably egalitarian structure.

If the structure of our community were only remarkable, however, this account would hardly be worthwhile. Here is a pattern that has been largely dismissed by social scientists and laymen. It has been dismissed partly because it has been overshadowed by important studies of social stratification, upward mobility, status symbols, power structures, and a heterogeneous, industrial society. Most sociologists argue, moreover, that stratification, which is at a minimum among the So-Sos, is a universal feature of social structures.

The So-So pattern has also been dismissed because it has been misunderstood. Its egalitarian ideals, accompanied by the processes and consequences involved in attaining them, are generally misinterpreted in the light of the "get-ahead" language of our day. Because we are immersed in our own achievement standards, we are poorly equipped for viewing the So-So community and are likely to respond to abbreviated descriptions of it with: "Ah yes, that is indeed a sick part of our society," or, "What can one do about such apathy?" As we shall see, however, the social structure of the So-Sos comes nearer supporting and being supported by our American dream of equal life chances than do most of the Jonesvilles of our nation.[1] The So-So structure makes sense in and of itself. It deserves a second look.

Far from seeking status symbols to enhance their positions, the So-Sos prefer to keep status differences to a minimum and have succeeded in doing so. In the following pages, the reader will learn some of the means by which the So-Sos break down class distinctions and discourage a relentless pursuit of success emblems.

These are not a peculiar nor isolated hill people who have somehow avoided western civilization. These are not the kinsfolk who remained behind because they lacked access to wealth or to natural endowments. These are, rather, the settlers who have "been there as long as anyone can remember," who chose to hold onto the same family land and the same family lines through a century and a half of intermarriage and residential stability. Nor have they relaxed their hold on what many Americans despairingly term "the good old ways" —ways of individual and community autonomy, ways of expressive, active concern for neighbor and kin.

No social scientist would look for a duplication of the So-So structure in a complex and occupationally-differentiated metropolitan center. The farther from this particular com-

1. W. Lloyd Warner and associates, *Democracy in Jonesville: A Study of Quality and Inequality.*

munity the writer goes, however, the clearer it is that there
are other So-So communities and, certainly, So-So values
sprinkled throughout industrial U.S.A. Then we are not accurate in identifying the salient characteristics of almost two
hundred million Americans as conspicuous display, a pro-
clivity for joining formal lodges and clubs, a dedication to
highly trained leadership and talent or to greater material ac-
quisition.

It would be pleasant, but not honest, to stop here. A part
of this book must deal with the problems and tragedies of
our egalitarian kinship community. The violence of one of
the most notorious trouble sections of Tennessee is geographically and functionally connected with at least half of this
area. Understanding that connection must await an understanding of kinship and community patterns.

These pages are written for those interested in structure
and strain within a somewhat extreme example of a familiar
kind of American community, where neighbor and friend
and kin and in-law are often the same.

The Deme Defined and Located

Family and community are one among the So-Sos. The
kinship network is dominant for such a system. That is,
the behavioral demands and consequences of kinship relations
take precedence over other community patterns. The condition intervening between kinship and other social networks
is local endogamy, the practice of choosing a marriage partner
within the bounds of the community. Endogamy must have
had its beginning with geographical isolation and valley
families' practice of marrying "conveniently," [2] and it per-
sists because it supposedly provides structural stability. It provides economic stability, since marrying into a neighboring
farm means access to land and consolidates and conserves

2. My husband has had a number of marriage candidates explain to
him, "Poor folks marry conveniently." A "convenient" wedding means
marrying a person who is easily accessible.

wealth. It provides cohesion insofar as marriage between persons allied by blood continually strengthens the kin network and reinforces the "mechanical solidarity" [3] that operates in such a system. And it gives personal satisfaction inasmuch as persons marry those whom they are expected to marry and whose way of life they share.

Where unilateral descent is absent, that is, where descent is not counted through only one parent's line, Murdock calls such an endogamous local group a "deme." [4] The word is especially appropriate for describing our community, for like "democracy" it comes from the Greek *demos* meaning the common people. In 508 B.C., Cleisthenes divided Attica into demes or townships, basing citizenship on residence instead of blood ties in order to break up control by certain aristocratic families. As used by Murdock, the deme is a kin group most comparable to a clan in size and in traditional bonds uniting its members. It is coextensive with community.

The deme or community thus chosen for theory testing and formulation is more than object or example.[5] It may be considered a sample, an empirical structural type, or subculture.

Containing sixty-four farm households, Applecross, Millstone, and Turnabout Hollow are valleys in the larger Tennessee Central Basin. They lie a few miles south of Nashville. Once dense in valuable timber and cane, with a bed of limestone beneath the surface, the soil produces some of the finest burley tobacco and widest variety of vegetables grown in

3. That solidarity which is formed by the collective sentiments of like persons and the solidarity based on the functional interdependence of unlike persons have been recognized as distinctively different since Durkheim discriminated between "mechanical" and "organic" solidarity. See Emile Durkheim, *The Division of Labor in Society* (1893), trans. George Simpson, pp. 70–132.

4. George P. Murdock, *Social Structure*, pp. 62–63, 159.

5. Conrad M. Arensberg, "The Community as Object and as Sample," *American Anthropologist*, LXIII, No. 2 (April 1961), 241–264.

temperate climate.[6] Ever-flowing springs and lush grass fields make the land good for livestock.

Separating Applecross and Millstone from Turnabout Hollow and other "Big Rook" territory is the Tennessee Valley Divide, which in this part of Kinbrace County is called Duck River Ridge. The Ridge provides a watershed for the Big Harpeth to the north and Duck River to the south, tributaries in turn for the Cumberland and Tennessee rivers.

It seemed wise to the writer to disregard the physical Ridge barrier and consider Applecross, Millstone, and Turnabout Hollow as one community, since the sixty-four farm families are closely interconnected by kinship, participation patterns, and norms. On these criteria, then, boundaries were established for a "complete" community, which constitutes thirty-three lower Ridge families, living in a natural geographical area and trading at Applecross country store, and thirty-one upper Ridge families with whom they have extensive contact. Throughout preliminary investigation, the proposed community boundaries appeared to hold, but data-gathering and analysis point to clear differences between Applecross-Millstone and Turnabout Hollow structures. These distinctions generate some of the most interesting theoretical questions of the study.

Conceptual Framework

Our deme differs primarily from many other American communities in that achievement criteria do not provide its basic structural framework. Accordingly, the goals of this study distinguish it from the traditional community monograph. It aims particularly at clarification of some effects

6. With the exception, perhaps, of the Nile Valley, no river bottom land benefits so much from phosphorus deposits of an overflowing river as does this land around Duck River, which is flooded and fertilized about every three years with valuable liquid phosphate. The phosphate is supposedly from the bone marrow of billions of dead sea animals that once lived in the sea which is now the Nashville Basin.

xxvi : Neighbor and Kin

which endogamy, bilateral descent, type of kinship solidarity, and closed or open social networks have on family and community organization. From a topical standpoint, discussions include such subjects as marriageability, inheritance, work-teams, and joking or violence among neighbor-kindred positions.

About a hundred years ago, through the historical and evolutionary writings of Morgan, Maine, Bachofen, M'Lennan, and before them of Millar (please see bibliography), kinship systems became recognized as scientifically important for understanding social organization. Since that time, leading anthropologists and sociologists have paid particular attention to kinship terminology and behavior. Such a list should include Rivers, Kroeber, Lowie, Malinowski, Radcliffe-Brown, Eggan, Lévi-Strauss, Evans-Pritchard, Leach, Parsons, Davis, Zimmerman, and Homans.

Social anthropologists have for the most part derived their theories of family and community organization from studies of non-Western unilateral descent systems which assign persons to either male or female lineages. Less is known of the effects of a kinship system which assigns relatives in terms of both parents. Societies based on the principles of bilateral descent, or the reckoning of kin status through both father and mother, are often described as "infinitely complex," or "loosely organized," or "unstructured." [7]

The present inquiry does not stand alone. Recent kinship studies have been made in Ireland by Arensberg and Kimball, in French Canada by Hughes and by Miner, in London by Young and Willmott and by Firth, and in Oxford by Mogey (please see bibliography). Many American community studies contain information on kin, and attention has been given lately to such single activities as visiting and help patterns among extended kin of the urban middle class. But the broad

7. Robert N. Pehrson, "Bilateral Kin Groupings as a Structural Type," *Journal of East Asiatic Studies*, III, No. 2 (January 1954), 199–203.

tendency has been either to point to those aspects of kinship which do not complement other American institutions or to substitute status for kinship.[8] The neglect of kin in sociological studies follows the stress placed on the nuclear rather than the extended family and the fact that occupation is the principal recruitment criterion for roles in industrial nations.

The prime and recurring problem of explaining social structure is approached here by examining a small, endogamous, bilateral system which substantially joins the two minimum structural features of all societies—kinship and residential community. The analysis focuses on the solution of two problems: the stratification pattern and the occasional outbursts of violence.

That such a focus calls for intellectual tools drawn from both sociology and social anthropology is not surprising. The close union of interests between the two disciplines, evident in past years, involves more than the fact that both now study literate societies. In addition to making holistic approaches to entire cultural systems, today's anthropologist also analyzes segments of society. And sociologists, while studying housing areas, fertility correlates, or juvenile delinquency, are more and more concerned with broad organizational patterns.

The present section is not intended to give a complete theoretical rationale for the problems these data present. The book follows the plan of joining some expository writing with specific facts, and there is an attempt in Part III to tie together and evaluate findings within a larger sociological and anthropological context. At this point, however, some background information may be useful to the reader.

In spite of its location in industrial U.S.A., where occupational and achievement criteria are strong, the Applecross-

8. Floyd Hunter, *Community Power Structure*; and W. Lloyd Warner and P. S. Lunt, *The Social Life of a Modern Community*.

xxviii : Neighbor and Kin

Millstone-Turnabout community is built mainly around ascriptive, or kinship, solidarity. It gives real substance to an ideal type of substructure which can and does exist in the midst of urban trends and which Parsons calls a "particularistic-ascriptive" structure.[9] In such a structure, behavior depends much more on *ascribed* characteristics over which persons have no control, such as sex, age, family connections, than it does on achieved characteristics for which persons have successfully competed. Moreover, each person expects certain treatment because of his *particular* relationship to another person rather than because of universal expectations applying to some common category. Also, in such a system, affection counts more than accomplishing a goal, and interest lies diffusely in the total person rather than in a specific role played at a specific time.

In other words, we can anticipate behavior in our community because of the degree to which certain ascriptive values have been institutionalized into roles: [10] The more attached to and conscious of kinship obligations persons are, the more concerned they are with particular rather than universal obligations, the more diffuse rather than specific are their personal attachments in these obligations, the more important quality rather than performance of individuals looms for them, the stronger an expressive rather than an instrumental approach appears, and the more often expressions take individual rather than collective form.

It is interesting that Parsons sees the particularistic-ascriptive community as the nearest possible antithesis to the national picture of modern America; for he gives America as an example of the "universalistic-achievement" type of structure, a system of rational economic pursuits in which goal achieve-

9. Talcott Parsons, *The Social System*, p. 198.

10. The statements in this paragraph and the preceding one make use of five pairs of role definitions as outlined by Parsons, *op. cit.*, pp. 58–67.

ment is accented, relations are instrumental, and roles are segregated, allowing fluidity in a stratified society.[11]

Detailed features of our community are suggested by the main characteristics of the particularistic-ascriptive pattern, as given by Parsons:

The whole community prefers a minimum of differentiation beyond that necessary for distinguishing roles by age, sex, and membership in a kin group.

Larger integrative and ecological structures are accepted as having positive functions when order is threatened but are operative only on such occasions.

The lack of emphasis on achievement inhibits the development of instrumental patterns. Work is considered a necessary evil. This is, above all, an aesthetic and expressive society, emphasizing such local creativity as singing or handicrafts.

The community has no incentive to disturb tradition; on the contrary, it has vested interest in the established order, which is its locus of authority. Morality, like work, is considered a necessary evil. Moral responsibility focuses to forestall the danger of unregulated expression which, through aggression and also through attachments that conflict with a given order, can be highly disruptive.

The society tends to be individualistic rather than collectivistic, but the individualism is concerned with expressive

11. Parsons describes two additional structural variations. One, the "universalistic-ascriptive" society, is illustrated by Nazi Germany. In it persons within a status-hierarchy are given assignments to bring about or defend an ideal state of affairs. The basic differences between the American pattern and the German one is that the first is individualistic with an economic accent, the second collectivistic with a political accent. Both patterns show internal strains between values and behavior. Classical China exemplifies the other type, the "particularistic-achievement" society, in which a strong collective moral code spells out each person's responsibility for the whole society, and in which activities are carried out diffusely with an overall concern for particular other persons. Kinship in this structure emphasizes ancestral continuity and traditionalism. *Op. cit.*, pp. 182–198.

interests and places little value on shaping the situation through achievement.[12]

An interesting epigram describing the mood of Parsons's particularistic-ascriptive society is given by a British scholar: "Leave us alone to enjoy ourselves in peace." [13]

12. Parsons, *op. cit.*, pp. 198–199.
13. W. J. H. Sprott, "Principia Sociologica," *The British Journal of Sociology*, III, No. 3 (September, 1952), 203–221.

Duck River Ridge, though the Ridge treaty was not made valid until years later. The largest portion of Mose's 1,100 acres lay north of the Military Line and south of the Ridge, a claim which might have been not only embarrassing but dangerous to make before the early part of the nineteenth century.

Some of the Huntlys living in the community today think that one of Mose's brothers may have come to the Ridge country some forty years before Mose. It is reasonable that the currently strong pattern of siblings (brothers and sisters) settling near one another was established in the valleys' first homesteading. This would also explain the presence of a nephew of Mose who married Mose's granddaughter, about two dozen of whose grandchildren and great-grandchildren now live in the community. At any rate, as early as 1823, Mose's name appears in a Kinbrace County newspaper. Though the handwriting was misread, the name is unmistakable and the location correct: "Strays: Taken up by Moses Hurthy, seen head of Millstone Creek, One Sorrell Mare, 15 years old." [2]

It is amazing that after 150 years so many details connected with this early kinsman's life are still alive in the eme's talk. A sample of the information follows.

Mose was a Scots immigrant. He had at least three occupations other than farming. He and his sons cut and sold grindstones and millstones at the old Harpeth Quarry at Applecross. His son's prices are given in an 1851 county newspaper: "Mill stone, three feet across the face, forty dollars— every inch longer, two dollars, across the face." [3] He planted an apple orchard on his hill and made enough brandy the basement of his home for a prosperous tavern across road, where Applecross Store now stands, and also for a nd tavern in Columbia, Tennessee. According to the

The Gazette, March 29, 1823. Drainage for the three valleys which he setting for this book is aided by three beautiful creeks.
Western Weekly Review, July 25, 1851.

Part 1. FAMILY

1. Early Family Structure

MUCH of the family structure of our com
probably persisted since Revolutionary
Eleven hundred acres of the productive land a
River Ridge was given as a Revolutionary Wa
continental soldier named Moses Huntly, wh
1742 to 1842. Mose was not alone. A large par
was settled soon after the Revolutionary War
of Scots-Irish and English origin came by wa
the Carolinas and Virginia to claim their F
ment grants across the mountains.

According to records in the National Arc
Mose did not move to his land immediately,
of a confusion of boundary lines between
the Chickasaw Indians. In the two years f
three different lines were established: th
Line" in 1783, abandoned because of In
established by informal treaty, also in 1
River Ridge the boundary; and the "Mil
dividing Tennessee equally east and w
as the midpoint between the north and s
cross and Millstone farmers point to tl
Hill as the place where the "Indians a
their land." Actually, the line the Ch

1. An open court record on April 8, 183
had resided in Rowan County, North Carolin
County in 1821.

British custom of having a sign over one's place of business, two wooden apples with crossed stems hung over the tavern near his home. This seems the likeliest guess as to how Apple-cross got its name. To his business, residents say, "men came from all around in orderly fashion." And, again in accordance with European interests, he dug two ponds in which he raised carp.

Everything did not go smoothly with Mose, however. Nearby slaves, to whom it was unlawful to sell brandy, crawled under his tavern at night, bored holes through the floor and barrels, conveniently plugging the barrels for return trips. When Mose went to switch the old and new brandy, the barrels were empty. Besides this, men seined the carp out of Mose's new ponds. So fond of his carp that he wouldn't even eat one himself, he was almost crazy with the idea of protecting them. Finally he and his boys cut locust trees, laid branches solid across the ponds, then wired them together so that it was impossible for anyone to seine; after this precaution, the old man went to bed and slept until noon the next day.

One of the incidents men enjoy telling is how Mose's granddaughter's husband joined the church and asked to be baptized in one of the ponds. The candidate for baptism was known over the community as "Uncle Herb," a rather rough and ready coffin maker. Right after the baptism, the dam to the pond broke, and one of Uncle Herb's sons-in-law made the statement that must have been repeated on the porch of the old country store a thousand times: "Uncle Herb's sins were so heavy they broke down the dam."

In the words of one of the oldest Huntlys in the county, "Granpappy Mose was a black-headed Scot; he lived to be a hundred and didn't have a dozen grey hairs." A favorite story, which residents say has been picked up from them for radio use, concerns a bearded farmer sitting on a fence crying. When a stranger asked his trouble, he replied, "My pappy whipped me." "What for?" the stranger asked. "For throwing rocks at my great-granpappy," said the old man. "You all sure do live long through here," the stranger exclaimed, "don't any of you ever die?" "No," the man drawled, "we just git so old we dry up into grasshoppers, and the turkeys eat us."

Recently, in the course of two hours of standing and talking outside the church, following an hour of revival preaching inside, a kinsman living near the Ridge told how his father at ninety-six walked some miles "to visit a corpse" just before he lay down and died himself. His father's two brothers lived to be ninety-five and ninety-seven. His grandfather at ninety-eight fell backward to his death as he carried tobacco strips up some rock steps.

Those who become childlike in their old age continue living at home near or occasionally with kin, who tease them more or less gently and explain to visitors, "She [or he] ain't got a care in the world." The old men usually have melodious voices, quick minds, remarkable memories, and are fascinating story tellers. And usually their bright eyes squint as they talk. Their wives sit more quietly, some of them occupied with spitting or with the at-times solemn, at-times jolly (but always unrewarding) task of brushing black and yellow Cornish-looking hens and their chicks away from the front door and porch. Sometimes a reassuring smile or deep-throated "thar" breaks through. One may wish very much to ally with these valley families, but "belonging" comes only through blood or marriage and long association. And the strongest alliances consist of all three bonds.

The Old Homestead

The first Applecross homestead is still the most imposing one in the valleys. It sits in the geographical center of Applecross-Millstone and plays an important part in the ethnic cohesiveness of the community. Residents have written poetry expressing their attachment to it. The home's history is significant to the deme, and a part of it would be meaningful to the next chapter on marriage and inheritance.

In valley terminology, "Negroes were still in harness" when Mose Huntly arrived in the Ridge area. By slave and son labor he built his home of blocks of yellow sandstone hauled from Groundhog Hollow in Corn Creek. It took seven years to complete the project. The blocks were three feet thick and so heavy four men could hardly lift one. A strong Negro called "Rock Dan" was overseer. Rock Dan's name is in the chimneys of the old house, and also in the chimneys of a number of other Kinbrace County homes built some 150 years ago. Dan saw that his stones were carefully cut and put together with a minimum of mortar so that his houses stand squarely to this day. The original inside plaster on the sandstone is in perfect condition. The house stands high off the ground for protection against Indians; it has high windows that are three feet in depth, a basement, and an attic with dormer windows. Near it is a fish pond, as old as the house, and locust trees, older.

The present owner and occupant of the house Mose built is his great-great-granddaughter, who married his great-grandson. Mose had six daughters and two sons. One son remained behind. The other, also named Mose (called in these pages the full name "Moses") willed that all his property be sold at his death, except for one acre of land embracing the family burying ground and for the dowry[4] which his wife brought to their marriage and which was to return to her. All money from the sale, the will specified, should be lent out and annual interest therefrom divided equally among the children.[5] The records show that what happened to the property then is the same as what has occurred to valley

4. "Dowry" is the term popularly used for the portion of land left to a man's widow.

5. One son never married. To him, Napoleon B. Huntly, Moses "bequeathed his riding horse, a sorrel, and saddle and bridle." "Pole" was the first man to put up a store in the community.

property time and again since—it was bought by the children and close kin.[6] About two hundred acres of it sold (at $22.00 an acre) to Moses's sister and her husband and to their son, who was Moses's son-in-law as well as his nephew. In the chart below, kin w and z bought a valuable third of the land. When w died, his son and later a grandson Ah came into possession of the homeplace.

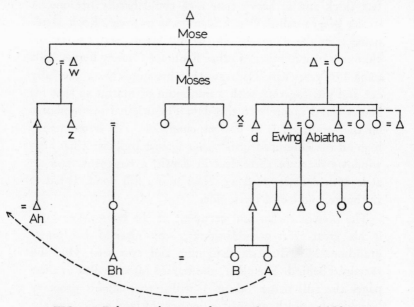

FIG. 1—*Relation of present homestead owner to builder.*

Note: In all of the kinship charts of this book, symbols are used to designate male, △ *; female,* ○ *; marriage,* = *; and sibling group,* ⌐——┐ *or* ⌐----┐ *.*

Moses had a second sister whose son married another of his daughters, but the couple divorced and no land was connected

6. In the nine pages of the Will Book on which are listed those who bought items and the five pages on which are listed those to whom Moses owed money, children's and siblings' and cousins' names are the most repeated. One hundred-dollar debt was paid to the deceased man's wife.

Part 1. FAMILY

1. Early Family Structure

MUCH of the family structure of our community has probably persisted since Revolutionary War days. Eleven hundred acres of the productive land around Duck River Ridge was given as a Revolutionary War grant to a continental soldier named Moses Huntly, whose dates are 1742 to 1842. Mose was not alone. A large part of Tennessee was settled soon after the Revolutionary War when families of Scots-Irish and English origin came by wagonloads from the Carolinas and Virginia to claim their Federal Government grants across the mountains.

According to records in the National Archives,[1] however, Mose did not move to his land immediately, probably because of a confusion of boundary lines between the settlers and the Chickasaw Indians. In the two years following the war, three different lines were established: the "Commissioners Line" in 1783, abandoned because of Indian claims; a line established by informal treaty, also in 1783, making Duck River Ridge the boundary; and the "Military Line" of 1784, dividing Tennessee equally east and west, using Slide Hill as the midpoint between the north and south borders. Applecross and Millstone farmers point to the rock wall on Slide Hill as the place where the "Indians and whites divided up their land." Actually, the line the Chickasaws observed was

1. An open court record on April 8, 1834, states that Moses Huntly had resided in Rowan County, North Carolina, before coming to Kinbrace County in 1821.

3

Duck River Ridge, though the Ridge treaty was not made valid until years later. The largest portion of Mose's 1,100 acres lay north of the Military Line and south of the Ridge, a claim which might have been not only embarrassing but dangerous to make before the early part of the nineteenth century.

Some of the Huntlys living in the community today think that one of Mose's brothers may have come to the Ridge country some forty years before Mose. It is reasonable that the currently strong pattern of siblings (brothers and sisters) settling near one another was established in the valleys' first homesteading. This would also explain the presence of a nephew of Mose who married Mose's granddaughter, about two dozen of whose grandchildren and great-grandchildren now live in the community. At any rate, as early as 1823, Mose's name appears in a Kinbrace County newspaper. Though the handwriting was misread, the name is unmistakable and the location correct: "Strays: Taken up by Moses Hurthy, seen head of Millstone Creek, One Sorrell Mare, 15 years old." [2]

It is amazing that after 150 years so many details connected with this early kinsman's life are still alive in the deme's talk. A sample of the information follows.

Mose was a Scots immigrant. He had at least three occupations other than farming. He and his sons cut and sold grindstones and millstones at the old Harpeth Quarry at Applecross. His son's prices are given in an 1851 county newspaper: "Mill stone, three feet across the face, forty dollars—for every inch longer, two dollars, across the face." [3] He planted an apple orchard on his hill and made enough brandy in the basement of his home for a prosperous tavern across the road, where Applecross Store now stands, and also for a second tavern in Columbia, Tennessee. According to the

2. *The Gazette*, March 29, 1823. Drainage for the three valleys which are the setting for this book is aided by three beautiful creeks.
3. *Western Weekly Review*, July 25, 1851.

British custom of having a sign over one's place of business, two wooden apples with crossed stems hung over the tavern near his home. This seems the likeliest guess as to how Apple-cross got its name. To his business, residents say, "men came from all around in orderly fashion." And, again in accordance with European interests, he dug two ponds in which he raised carp.

Everything did not go smoothly with Mose, however. Nearby slaves, to whom it was unlawful to sell brandy, crawled under his tavern at night, bored holes through the floor and barrels, conveniently plugging the barrels for return trips. When Mose went to switch the old and new brandy, the barrels were empty. Besides this, men seined the carp out of Mose's new ponds. So fond of his carp that he wouldn't even eat one himself, he was almost crazy with the idea of protecting them. Finally he and his boys cut locust trees, laid branches solid across the ponds, then wired them together so that it was impossible for anyone to seine; after this precaution, the old man went to bed and slept until noon the next day.

One of the incidents men enjoy telling is how Mose's granddaughter's husband joined the church and asked to be baptized in one of the ponds. The candidate for baptism was known over the community as "Uncle Herb," a rather rough and ready coffin maker. Right after the baptism, the dam to the pond broke, and one of Uncle Herb's sons-in-law made the statement that must have been repeated on the porch of the old country store a thousand times: "Uncle Herb's sins were so heavy they broke down the dam."

In the words of one of the oldest Huntlys in the county, "Granpappy Mose was a black-headed Scot; he lived to be a hundred and didn't have a dozen grey hairs." A favorite story, which residents say has been picked up from them for radio use, concerns a bearded farmer sitting on a fence crying. When a stranger asked his trouble, he replied, "My pappy whipped me." "What for?" the stranger asked. "For

throwing rocks at my great-granpappy," said the old man. "You all sure do live long through here," the stranger exclaimed, "don't any of you ever die?" "No," the man drawled, "we just git so old we dry up into grasshoppers, and the turkeys eat us."

Recently, in the course of two hours of standing and talking outside the church, following an hour of revival preaching inside, a kinsman living near the Ridge told how his father at ninety-six walked some miles "to visit a corpse" just before he lay down and died himself. His father's two brothers lived to be ninety-five and ninety-seven. His grandfather at ninety-eight fell backward to his death as he carried tobacco strips up some rock steps.

Those who become childlike in their old age continue living at home near or occasionally with kin, who tease them more or less gently and explain to visitors, "She [or he] ain't got a care in the world." The old men usually have melodious voices, quick minds, remarkable memories, and are fascinating story tellers. And usually their bright eyes squint as they talk. Their wives sit more quietly, some of them occupied with spitting or with the at-times solemn, at-times jolly (but always unrewarding) task of brushing black and yellow Cornish-looking hens and their chicks away from the front door and porch. Sometimes a reassuring smile or deep-throated "thar" breaks through. One may wish very much to ally with these valley families, but "belonging" comes only through blood or marriage and long association. And the strongest alliances consist of all three bonds.

The Old Homestead

The first Applecross homestead is still the most imposing one in the valleys. It sits in the geographical center of Applecross-Millstone and plays an important part in the ethnic cohesiveness of the community. Residents have written poetry expressing their attachment to it. The home's history

is significant to the deme, and a part of it would be meaningful to the next chapter on marriage and inheritance.

In valley terminology, "Negroes were still in harness"
when Mose Huntly arrived in the Ridge area. By slave and
son labor he built his home of blocks of yellow sandstone
hauled from Groundhog Hollow in Corn Creek. It took
seven years to complete the project. The blocks were three
feet thick and so heavy four men could hardly lift one. A
strong Negro called "Rock Dan" was overseer. Rock Dan's
name is in the chimneys of the old house, and also in the
chimneys of a number of other Kinbrace County homes built
some 150 years ago. Dan saw that his stones were carefully
cut and put together with a minimum of mortar so that his
houses stand squarely to this day. The original inside plaster
on the sandstone is in perfect condition. The house stands
high off the ground for protection against Indians; it has high
windows that are three feet in depth, a basement, and an
attic with dormer windows. Near it is a fish pond, as old as
the house, and locust trees, older.

The present owner and occupant of the house Mose built
is his great-great-granddaughter, who married his great-
grandson. Mose had six daughters and two sons. One son
remained behind. The other, also named Mose (called in these
pages the full name "Moses") willed that all his property
be sold at his death, except for one acre of land embracing the
family burying ground and for the dowry[4] which his wife
brought to their marriage and which was to return to her.
All money from the sale, the will specified, should be lent
out and annual interest therefrom divided equally among the
children.[5] The records show that what happened to the
property then is the same as what has occurred to valley

---

4. "Dowry" is the term popularly used for the portion of land left to
a man's widow.

5. One son never married. To him, Napoleon B. Huntly, Moses "bequeathed his riding horse, a sorrel, and saddle and bridle." "Pole" was
the first man to put up a store in the community.

property time and again since—it was bought by the children and close kin.[6] About two hundred acres of it sold (at $22.00 an acre) to Moses's sister and her husband and to their son, who was Moses's son-in-law as well as his nephew. In the chart below, kin w and z bought a valuable third of the land. When w died, his son and later a grandson Ah came into possession of the homeplace.

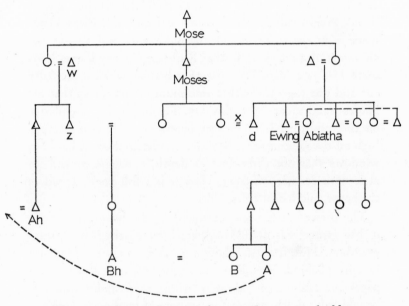

FIG. 1—*Relation of present homestead owner to builder.*

Note: In all of the kinship charts of this book, symbols are used to designate male, △ *; female,* ○ *; marriage,* = *; and sibling group,* ⌐—┬—┐ *or* ⌐- - - -┐ .

Moses had a second sister whose son married another of his daughters, but the couple divorced and no land was connected

6. In the nine pages of the Will Book on which are listed those who bought items and the five pages on which are listed those to whom Moses owed money, children's and siblings' and cousins' names are the most repeated. One hundred-dollar debt was paid to the deceased man's wife.

with this marriage. Descendants say it's funny they couldn't get along, for they were "own cousins." [7] Besides d, Moses's sister had three children who married siblings from a neighboring family. One of these, a son named Ewing, started for Texas with the wagon trains in October of 1850 with his wife Abiatha and their six children. En route in Upsid County, Texas, Ewing died. Abiatha turned back toward Applecross with her six small children, and she died at Smithland, Tennessee. The children were brought back to Applecross, their guardianship contested in court after distant kin above the Ridge tried to claim them, and were reared by Abiatha's family. Daughter A of one of the children married Ah (her second cousin once removed) and is the present occupant of the Huntly homestead. Her sister B married Ah's first cousin once removed (a third-cousin union). At present, Ah and Bh still have the most cherished land holdings, though the size of their farms is consistent with the size of other valley holdings.

The diagram is of interest because it shows the relation of the homestead owners to the original Mose; it suggests how marriage choice, divorce, residence and descent norms can affect the fate of a particular piece of land; and it reflects several important marriage practices.

7. In proper anthropological, although not common valley, terminology, this paper uses "first cousins" or "own cousins" to refer to children of siblings, "second cousins" as children of first cousins, "third cousins" as children of second cousins, and so on. A certain "cousin once removed" is a child of that particular cousin.

2. Marriage, Residence, and Inheritance

ON several informal occasions valley residents defined most accurately basic structural principles of their community. One such statement plainly illustrates the positive gradients of propinquity and kinship affecting marriage choices.[1] An older kinsman, who had walked across the road to see who was visiting his brother, gave the following account.

Say, once I walked over the Ridge to see a man about shoeing my horse. When I got thar, he looked real happy, and he says, "Say, I married me a Huntly." I didn't even know he'd been courtin', but I thought a minute; then I says, "Yeah? and I know who it was—either _____ or _____." That surprised him, 'cause it was the first gal I named. "How'd you know?" he asked. "Simple," I says, "one lives the closest, and the other's most kin."

Residential propinquity and distance from sibship could not be stated more clearly.

Cousin marriages and the tendency for brothers and sisters to choose mates who are themselves either siblings or first cousins are evident in Figure 1. These patterns are discussed more fully in the last sections of this chapter and of Chapter IV. In the valleys studied, ties between siblings and cousins are especially strong. A function of multiple marriages between sibling groups (such as involved Ewing and Abiatha

---

1. Murdock wrote of the strength of propinquity and kinship as mate-selection determinants in the absence of strong negative sanctions against them. George P. Murdock, *Social Structure*, pp. 318–320.

and their siblings) is to give structural continuity to the strong collateral cohesion that already exists among brothers, sisters, and first cousins. For siblings of one group to marry siblings of another is considered ideal and provides security in times of emergency. There is a saying in the valley that double first cousins are really closer than brothers and sisters. And, of course, in the Anglo-Saxon sibship identical kinship status is held only by full brothers and sisters, double first cousins, or half brothers and sisters whose unshared parents are full siblings; these persons alone share all the same kindred.

The close tie between collateral kinsfolk—or the lack of it between lineal or vertical kinsfolk—is seen too in the universal valley practice of "running away" to marry, the place of destination being the magistrate, or "square" (squire) as he is often called, just over the Ridge.[2] Typical answers to the question of who helped arrange for the marriage are, "We run away," "There was no one but us," "We just married on off," "There was just me and him." Upon being asked whom he told first when he decided to marry, one man grinned, and pointed to his wife. "Her," he said, "she was fifteen. We run off. But after we come home her pappy said, 'You could of took her long ago if you'd wanted her.' " Another man just didn't know what the world was coming to—it was getting harder and harder to get married, and finally "folks won't be able to marry at all."

The runaway phenomenon seems strange, since young people marry endogamously and apparently those whom the deme expects them to marry. The typical responses quoted above were often followed by, "But everyone knew about us." Two men mentioned an agreement of long standing that their own girl cousin should prepare their wedding supper and be hostess to them and their bride-elect on the

2. This indeed is marrying most "conveniently" and economically; nor does it invite the social cost of showing favoritism in selecting the bridal party from among a community of kin.

wedding night, and although these men "ran off" to marry, the dinner date was kept. Several mentioned that a sibling or cousin helped them "slip off," and one man even named a girlfriend as helping. In general, sanctions of collateral relatives are more important to the marriage event than sanctions of lineal relatives, and the runaway pattern seems merely a ceremonial defiance to parental control.

Another condition in Figure 1 worth noting is that Ah is one generation older than A. An 1858 county news edition[3] recommended a difference of seven years between husband and wife, "since there is a difference of seven years in the stamina of the constitutions, the symmetry of the form, etc." According to the 1880 census, for the forty-eight couples in the two districts comprising Turnabout Hollow, Applecross, and Millstone, the average age was forty-two for the married man and thirty-six for the married woman, an age gap of six years. At present, Applecross-Millstone couples range from their early twenties to their late seventies, with fifty-four the average age of the married man in the community and forty-eight the average age of the married woman. (This excludes the one widower and two widows there.)

The average age at first marriage for the sixty-two adults in Applecross-Millstone is twenty-three for the man and seventeen for the woman, an age gap still of six years. Not only are grooms still ideally older than their brides, but early marriage age for the woman is supported idealistically as well as in practice. As one informant asserted: "Lots of girls marry too old. There are always divorces when girls wait so long. Girls who marry young do better." The divorce shown in Figure 1 is one of only twelve identified in more than two thousand names in the genealogies, and age is actually not a factor. Three of the twelve divorces involve first cousins. Five occurred below and seven above the Ridge. Six divorced

3. *Western Weekly Review,* March 18, 1858.

spouses came from a different county and returned to their
homes after the divorces. The most significant aspect of the
twelve divorces is that four family names are involved in
eleven of them.

As expected for an area with strict sex norms and delayed
male marriages, at least one female prostitute for each of four
generations was identified. The prostitutes have come predominantly from two family groups and have lived just at
the edge of the community. The effect of prostitution is to
stop kin knowledge. One woman, whose mother and mother's
sister both played the role, could not give any of her grandparents' names. She explained, "I didn't have no father,
honey; that nearly kilt me."

Finally, Figure 1 suggests a property advantage in close
and lasting kin marriages. In an endogamous bilateral system
there is not such clear and consistent relation between
property transference, residence rules, and mate selection
as there is for a unilocal unilineal society where residence and
descent rules are set according to only one parent's lines.
But this is not to say that marriage, residence, and inheritance
do not qualify each other to a significant degree in our deme.
The relation of the factors is implicit in three principles
operating in the transference of property, principles which
sometimes contradict one another in valley practice.

Property Transference

The first principle is that farm ownership may be readily
shifted in order that a couple may have sufficient adjacent
acreage to have a comfortable subsistence. The second is seen
in the effort to divide inheritance equally among bodily heirs.
These principles are often cross-cut by a third principle: it is
desirable for land to remain in the same family name.

Although property in the area changes easily from the possession of one nuclear family to another, it remains generation after generation within the same valley lines. This is sort

of an extended and untimed "fruit basket turnover." [4] The same families change places often but continue to fill the positions, and persons who are left out of one play may wait for positions in the next or, on rare occasions, drop out of the game entirely.[5] Auctions are a recurring means for transference of the property. For more than one hundred years neighbors and close and distant kin have been purchasing land and smaller possessions at the time of a resident's death.[6] The fruit-basket-turnover pattern facilitates the most advantageous use of the deme's land within each generation, and the practice of auctioning helps give siblings and other members of the family equal advantage in securing the land.

It is often the case that a farm will retain its original family name, being called the "Smith Farm," for example, even though the owners have not been named Smith for years. The third principle is seen at work here in the likelihood that when this farm is put up for auction, non-Smiths will hold back and let a Smith buy it. One informant told how his family had "required" land to stay in the possession of sons, or of daughters whose married and maiden names were the same. Another informant said laughingly that a fellow once asked a neighbor of his, "How come you got all this property? Do you all marry kin?" "Yeah," the man replied, "brothers marry even." The informant then told seriously how a girl cousin of his was about to marry a "stranger" from a nearby community rather than some kinsman with her name. The girl's siblings gathered around her and advised, "Sis, we know you're marrying a man with property, but you are losing

4. In a game familiar to American children, each child is seated in a circle and is given the name of a different fruit. When "It" calls the names of several fruits the respective players must change seats and "It" tries to get a seat in the switch. The signal for everyone to change is, "Fruit basket turn over."

5. Prostitution, mentioned above, could be a type of "drop out," if no more men in one's generation (and therefore no more land) are available.

6. County Will Books dating from 1855.

your great-grandfather's land," and the girl broke her relations with the stranger.

The runaway marriage pattern was mentioned in the preceding section. Obviously parents do not arrange marriages along the Ridge, as they do in rural Ireland, in order that adjacent land can be worked by one family. If parents do not have the power to assign sons or daughters in marriage and thereby see that property is advantageously transferred, what are some of the ways the deme and the siblings themselves have of making peaceful and profitable settlements? The practice of "buying out" brothers and sisters is one of the most common ways and is usually handled through auctions. If a person moves in the house with or moves near aged parents and remains there until their death, that person has earned the right to "buy out" his siblings and also to the possession of the dowry. Or, if a particular division for the property is specified, then the children buy or trade for or marry into acreage adjoining their respective shares.

One respondent observed that the son who stayed at home the longest, or sons and daughters who married spouses living nearby, were likely to end up with the family land. She and her husband's families have both been in the community for five generations. Her parents requested that their youngest son, who had remained at home longer than the other children, "buy out" his siblings. Her husband's parents divided their land equally before they died, so that each couple had "part of the original land grant." Her husband and his siblings then each bought enough adjoining acres to complete their farms.

Auctions

The part that auctions play in this system is theoretically important, for it is a link between ecological factors and the social systems of the community and the kindred. Normally, after a couple dies their children have all the property auctioned and divide the money equally. The money is then used to buy back the home property or to buy other local real estate. The children let it be known which one or ones want the land, and there is a community-wide understanding as to who should get what property. The auction, then, is a community event through which the deme exercises control in a "wise" redistribution of property; through the auction, the community has the last word on price and buyer of valley land.

Let us look at an actual case above the Ridge in which a group of five siblings (three brothers and two sisters) were heirs to their grandfather's land that had been in the possession of their bachelor uncle who died. The siblings put the sixty-five-acre farm up for auction, and two of the brothers let it be known that they wanted the land. The older brother already had a farm, including part of his parents' land. The younger brother Bill was a tenant and community talk favored him, but he lacked the means to buy the land. Bill's second cousin and a group of more distant kin went to see a banker and offered to stand with Bill in a debt for the amount they thought would be a winning bid.

Some eighty men and women were present at the auction. A neighbor to the piece of property opened the bid, after which Bill and his older brother were the only bidders. The older brother's bid went beyond what Bill was able to borrow. At this point, the auctioneer called an intermission, saying, "You folks walk all over the land. We want everyone to be sure and everyone to bid who wants to bid." During the intermission, three local residents who hauled walnut timber stepped to Bill's side and expressed a desire for the cedar on the property being auctioned, offering to pay for it immediately if Bill raised the bid. He did so and was the successful bidder. The older brother apparently holds no grudge against Bill or the community. He and Bill are neighbors and are together daily. Their children are especially close.

The role played by the auctioneer in this and other local auctions is highly significant. He is a puppet for the community. He is sensitive to the directions in which the deme wishes to move. He prides himself on recognizing such signs as a lifted finger or a side glance. Often he says, "All secret bids will be honored" or "I have a very sharp eye, and I will see you if you give me a secret sign." This, of course, gives the auctioneer the freedom to acknowledge or reject bids without the crowd's even knowing it. He also has the freedom to call intermissions when things are not going right or to speed up at the opportune times. Often the auctioneer is a real estate dealer himself, knows the assets of men in the deme, and is able to suggest ways to turn these to the financial advantage of a favored bidder.

Strangers occasionally attend a local auction such as the one described and are sometimes successful bidders on small items. By valley terms, these are not "rank strangers," for a "rank stranger" is a person never seen before. These "strangers" have been seen numerous times at county-seat auctions. If a stranger bids on land, the auctioneer often says he has a "secret bidder" who will top the stranger's bid, or he speaks to the stranger at intermission, saying there is a sentiment attached to the land and that the children will give much more than it is worth. Sometimes he makes a public plea as: "Here is a sister who wants to live by a sister." If the stranger should persist, the land may be withdrawn, or the stranger may even be involved in a brawl. Everyone in attendance is made aware of the importance of neighbors, and outsiders sense that they would not fit into the community. One outsider admitted, "I wouldn't think of buying that land. I would feel continually embarrassed like I was living in someone else's home where I didn't belong."

A doctor in one of the valleys whom 90 percent of the families use recently had an auction to sell off his dairy herd in order to go into beef cattle. The church served lunch for his auction, and it drew more than three hundred persons. About half of his cows were bought locally and the other half by "strangers" who had heard of the sale through county-seat auction news.

Couples in Turnabout Hollow attend fairly regularly the two auctions in the county seat each Saturday. At these auctions household and farming equipment and stock are sold. Some Ridge men buy pieces of equipment at the auctions and act almost as retailers for the community, making it a point, for example, to keep an extra plow in their barn. One such man is referred to as "sort of a trader" and is used widely by those farmers who seldom drive into town. The man, his wife, his cousin, and his cousin's wife often go to the auctions together. Valley residents know the history of merchandise on which they bid. The cousin's wife is proud of a dresser she bought at a county-seat auction; the dresser came from her great-aunt's home.

Some of the main features of Ridge auctions may be summarized as follows: They are very local in nature. Ten miles is considered too far for Ridge folks to travel to an auction if it is beyond the boundary they recognize, as in the flats, but some of them travel as far as fifteen miles to one in the county seat or in the hills, especially along the Ridge. Auctions, something like a county fair, are a time for sociability. It is common for a church or community group to serve dinner at an auction. At one which the writer's family attended, equipment was auctioned in the morning and cattle were to be auctioned after lunch. The veterinarian's blood tests located one diseased cow in the herd to be sold, and a three-day quarantine had to be put on the herd until the owner could get a bill of good health. The auctioneer knew this but said nothing about it until after dinner. As he explained later to the men, who took it good-naturedly, "I couldn't let the ladies down who had fixed all this delicious food." [7]

The auctioneer comes from the county seat or from a

7. It is probable that the owners and other local persons knew of the disease and that this is another case wherein the auctioneer served as a puppet for the community.

smaller town nearby and knows the locality and customs well. For large items, especially land, the auctioneer always comes to the valley location. Owners have often expressed preferences as to who should buy, and these preferences, as well as the preferences of the community, are well known to the auctioneer. The deme, through the formal process of bidding, sets the "fair" price for the land, giving a safe clearance ground and guarding against hard feelings between the sellers and buyers. The auction itself is thus a scapegoat device. Its formal front is that each person in attendance has an equal chance to bid and buy. The kinship structure affects the outcome as certain courtesies are extended close relatives (as in the example of Bill and his brother). A sense of fairness affects the outcome as the deme considers the needs and means of the preferred buyer.

Auctions function most effectively to maintain sibling solidarity after parents' death: important items such as houses and land involve a delicate interplay between collaterals, most often siblings, with the deme mediating through the auction process. Auctions also serve as an intergenerational device; where smaller items are concerned a generation of older men counsels with a generation of younger ones, in this case using the auctioneer himself as mediator. For these cheaper items, for example, old men gather around the young farmer and give him advice on what he needs, such as, "Better buy that field drag, son, can't make another for $2.00." Usually one can buy a second-hand tobacco setter, the most expensive tobacco tool, for less than $45.00. (Or a man may have access to a work-team's setter or set his tobacco by hand.) He can usually buy a disk plow for $10.00 and a harrow for $2.00.

Auctions, therefore, serve an important economic purpose. They keep agricultural tools active and circulating. They direct cheap and usable equipment into the hands of young men getting started in farming. Furniture, household equipment, hand tools, cattle, haying equipment, mules, harnesses are all secured in this way. Members of the deme are thereby discouraged from hoarding excess equipment and "white elephants." Auctions thus implement property transference in a way that maintains the deme's ecological system and satisfies family relations.

Residence Practices

When Applecross and Millstone couples were asked how they came to live in their present house, 45 percent said it was the husband's or wife's inheritance, and 55 percent had bought from cousins, uncles, or other kin. One man who had lived a mile from his wife before marriage sold his own inheritance to his brothers in order to buy land next to hers. Another worked several years before marriage for his wife's uncle with whom his orphaned wife lived; then he and his wife remained on the place after the uncle died. A sixty-year-old man who had always lived in the same hollow said, "Why, I holped my father build this house when I was ten years old." His wife put her own home up for auction when her husband bought out his brothers and sisters. A neighbor bought a farm forty-three years ago from his wife's uncle (who had previously purchased it from a cousin) in order to be near a first cousin who bought the adjoining farm at the same time.

All but two Applecross-Millstone couples said they lived with some of their kin for a while immediately following marriage. Usually this was for only a few weeks. In two-thirds of the cases the short residence was with the husband's kin. One wife told how she ran off at eighteen and married the twenty-four-year-old man she had been seeing for seven years. Thinking her family would be unhappy about the marriage, the couple went to his family's home. After three days her parents sent word that everything was all right, and they returned to live permanently with her parents. With satisfaction she added: "Those were the only three days I ever lived anywhere but right here." Her inheritance was her birthplace and only homeplace. Her older brother across the road also lives in the home that was his birthplace and inheritance; a third brother lives about half a mile away in a hollow he bought from his wife's kin; and a fourth brother lives about two miles away on land that was his wife's inheritance. These farms are approximately eighty acres each.

Enough has been written at this point to illustrate some of the relations between property, residence, and mate selection and the advantages of alliances with kin and close neighbors.[8] It is time to look at the institution of cousin marriages.

Cousin Marriages

> Had you ever a cousin, Tom!
> And did your cousin sing!
> Sisters we've all by the dozen, Tom,
> But a cousin's a different thing.

A cousin is a different thing. Who is there that has not had a cousin who almost set him mad? They are privileges—these cousins are. They are so near sisters that they think they can treat one as they please, and then sometimes they get caught themselves. There's the rub. They are wild, romping animals, and do just as they please with perfect propriety. "Oh! it's only my cousin," is a settler as plump as "Oh, it's only my husband," in the play. They take great liberties sometimes. They want a beau; they call upon their cousin, poor fellow, and he must go. She is led on from one foolish speech to another, until both their heads become thickened up with the ideas of connubial felicity and the next thing that is heard of them is the announcement.[9]

In the words of a recently deceased and much-quoted kinswoman, "All these folks married their first cousins. I always heard they wouldn't be smart but look at them." And one looks at them to find three brothers who are talented preachers and a fourth brother mimicking their sermons word

8. Further information on residence factors before and after marriage is given in Chapter Five under the subheading "Boundary Maintenance."
9. *Western Weekly Review*, December 20, 1850.

for word to the delight of all around, self-taught poets and artists whose paintings hang in nationally known collections,[10] the most engaging and enthusiastic story-tellers anywhere in Tennessee, musicians who play and sing with individual and expressive styles—healthy, intelligent, and happy people.

As the 1850 article would lead us to believe, it is indeed the girl, rather than the boy, who takes liberties and makes advances in valley cousin contacts. The communication between one thirteen-year-old girl and her sixteen-year-old cousin, who live half a mile from each other and have played together always, has changed noticeably from a rowdy play relationship to a dignified joking relationship. The boy's joking is straightforward, the girl's more subtle. Some dozen relatives were visiting in the girl's front room, and the talk was of old times. The boy said to his cousin, "Do you still have that old doll house?" Her reply was coy and made his cheeks blush red: "Yes, do you want to play house?"

In an area where cousins grow up together much like siblings yet realize in adolescence that courtship is a possibility, behavior patterns change noticeably overnight. The result may be a joking relationship or a clear-cut instrumental one such as the long-standing agreements to help in marriage arrangements. The pattern of cousins marrying siblings, that is, for a boy and girl who are own cousins to marry a girl and a boy who are brother and sister, is significant here in that it is just a step away from cousins marrying one another; it involves standing together in choosing a mate and is thus an expression of own cousins' intent in maintaining a close sibling-like relation. The own cousins thereby achieve sibling-in-law statuses through their spouses.

A few generations ago first-cousin marriages were believed

10. Such collections include those of Hume Cronyn, Jessica Tandy, and Victor Borge.

biblical [11] and were practiced with religious passion. In a selected diagram of Huntly lines given below, those with the Huntly surname are marked with an "H." It can be seen that four of HH's children and four pairs of his grandchildren married first cousins. Three Huntly daughters married their father's sisters' sons. Two sets of mothers and sons married first cousins. For five marriages in three succeeding generations (shown on the far right of the diagram) no new surname was introduced. One kinsman volunteered with penetrating valley humor, "My pappy was a Huntly, and my mammy was a Huntly. Guess that makes me full-blooded." He grinned, "Speck I orta be reg'stered."

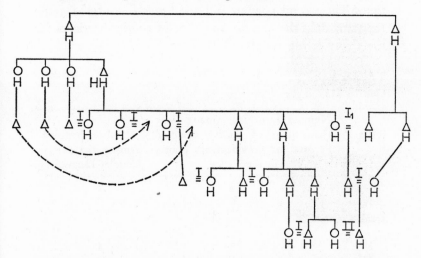

FIG. 2—*Selected genealogy showing close-cousin marriages. Roman numerals stand for the type of cousin, and the subscript "1" for "once removed."*

Though first-cousin marriages are still not uncommon and even continue to be the mode for several family lines above

11. And they are indeed biblical. Abraham, who himself married a half sister, sent for his brother's son's daughter as a fit wife for his son Isaac (Isaac's first cousin once removed). First-cousin marriage is legal today in the State of Tennessee.

the Ridge, valley mates today are not as often first cousins
and first cousins once removed as they are second cousins,
second cousins once removed, and third cousins. Not many
third-cousin-once-removed or fourth-cousin marriages can
be identified, which is to be expected in such a small population.

Given below in table and graph forms are the cousin
marriages counted in the genealogies of thirty couples in the
area studied most closely. The first column of the table and
the upper line of the graph represent the number and type
of cousin marriages found for the thirty couples and their
ascendants living in the valley during four preceding generations. The second column and the lower line of the graph
represent only the number and type of cousin marriages for
the thirty living couples themselves.

TABLE 1

Cousin Marriages

Type	Number Identified Among Four Generations of Thirty Couples' Parents and Grandparents Living in the Valley	Number Identified Among the Thirty Couples Themselves
I	10	1
I_1	6	2
total	16	3
II	9	5
II_1	5	4
total	14	9
III	6	5
III_1	1	1
total	7	6
IV	1	1
TOTAL	38	19

Note: Roman numerals stand for the type of cousin and the subscript "1" for
"once removed."

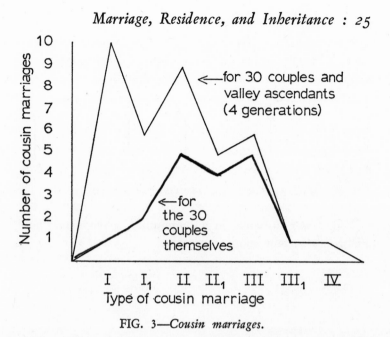

FIG. 3—*Cousin marriages.*

Prevalence of first-cousin marriages is one of the things for which Duck River Ridge provides a dividing line. There are more close marriages today among families north of the valley divide. Since this section was settled earlier than the lower Indian territory and is closer to good roads leading to the county seat and to Nashville, the fact is puzzling. One possible explanation is that in moonshine operations, common above the Ridge, there are special advantages in closed corporate family groups as contrasted to a close corporate deme group in the other area. This will be discussed in Chapter V. Fourteen children of one current sibling group over the Ridge are married to first cousins. Ten different unions, or roughly between a third and half of the total marriages of these six siblings' offspring, involve only two family names. If we let A stand for one family surname in the following chart and B for another, we see that in six cases an A married a B and in four cases an A married an A. One lower Ridge woman commented, "They all married up like that. I said if I couldn't marry someone not kin to me, I wouldn't marry." Her definition of kin evidently did not extend past second cousin, as she married her third cousin.

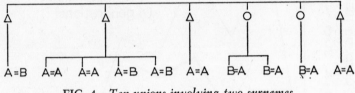

FIG. 4—*Ten unions involving two surnames.*

With fewer surnames in a community, given names and nicknames become more important.

3. Names and Titles

THE strength of collateral ties is reflected also in naming patterns. Couples more often name an offspring for one another or for their brothers and sisters than they do for parents or grandparents. Current naming patterns in the genealogies reveal 17 cases in which parents named their children for one of the parents' siblings, 29 cases in which parents named their children for themselves, 15 cases for the parents' parents, and 3 for the parents' grandparents. Thus 72 percent of the offspring are named for parents or parents' siblings and 23 percent for older ancestors.

A consequence of married couples' sharing ancestors with multiple namesakes is seen in the fact that at least a dozen persons interviewed have spouses with the same given name as one of their siblings. For example, one woman's husband and brother are both named Maynard; another's husband and sister are both named Leslie.

The given names in the chart below illustrate the confusion that can result in a closed corporate genealogy. Consider Martha. Martha's father and brother and husband were named William and Willie and Will. Another brother had a son he called William and a daughter-in-law named Willie. One of Martha's first cousins married a Willie. Another first cousin named her son Willie and still another had a daughter who married a William. Martha has seven additional second and third cousin Will's and William's not shown in the chart. Or consider Martha's two brothers, Willie and Odie. Willie

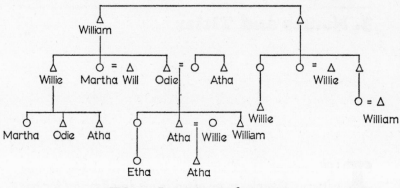

FIG. *5—Repetitions in first names.*

named two of his children Martha and Odie after his siblings, and he called another son Atha. Odie named one of his sons Atha after his wife's brother and another William after either his own brother or his father; Odie's son Atha in turn named his only boy Atha, and his sister named her only child (a daughter) Etha. To add to the confusion in names, Etha's mother lives across the road from Etha and her family, who live just adjoining the two Athas.

In another case Andy Lee has an own cousin Annie D., a cousin Earl Dee who married Lee, and a cousin Annie Lee who married Ad and has a sister who named her daughter Addie. Andy Lee named his girl Andra Dee.

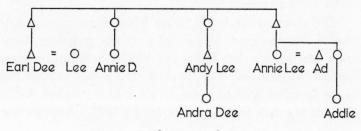

FIG. *6—Similarities in first names.*

The lack of sex differentiation seen in these illustrations of valley naming patterns is structurally important for a particularistic-ascriptive society in which distinctions of every type are minimized.

The fact that women in the area above the Ridge are frequently given men's names sometimes results in a husband and wife having identical first names. Or the names may be almost identical, since many names are changed only one letter when they are transferred from one sex to another, as Cora to Core, Leo to Cleo or to Lee, Doris to Dorris, Jessie to Chessie, Allen to Ellen.

Another interesting occurrence is for one spouse's surname to be identical with the other spouse's given name, reflecting cases in which parents call an offspring by one of their grandmothers' maiden names. For example, Dawn Carter was called by the maiden surname of her mother's grandmother Bell Dawn. Dawn married George, a second cousin once removed. Since George's father's father was Bell's brother, George had their surname, and his bride became Dawn Dawn. There are two cases in which a woman's surname is used as a given name for both granddaughters and grandsons.

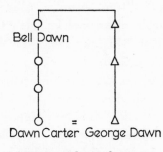

Bell Dawn

Dawn Carter = George Dawn

FIG. 7—*Identical names.*

Nicknames

Valley names are not without humor as well as confusion. One informant told of the indecision of her neighbors in naming a new baby. The husband would say, "You name her" and the wife, "You name her," and the little girl became "Namer." Another family had a Columbus called "Lum," a

Napoleon B. called "Pole" and a Washington called "Colonel."
Some given names are shortened the same way for each genera-
tion. Frances is always "Fannie," Priscilla Elizabeth "Ella,"
Kathleen "Cat," Sarah Elizabeth "Sally."

Nicknames and abbreviated names have obvious utility
in such a system. If more than one living person has the same
name, surname nicknames may be used.[1] Three Mose Huntlys
become Mose "Fiddler," Mose "Sledge," and Mose "Stick."
Or a person with a name overlap is identified by spouse as
"Mary's Mose" or "Will's Sally" or if unmarried, by parent,
as "Mose's Mose" or "Mary's Sally."

More than just utility, however, nicknames seem to distinguish between those who "belong" and those outside the
deme's boundary. Even the churches have nicknames, as
"Slide Church" and "Mud Hill Church." Though some nicknames sound cruel, residents think of them as titles of endear-
ment. For example, even at the time of family tragedy, a man
who is nicknamed for a serious defect is still addressed tenderly
by everyone as "Flop Ear." Other male nicknames are "Nig,"
"Bat," "Big Hip," "Iron Arm," "Alligator," "Creep,"
"Turtlehead." Female nicknames include "Doodie," "Bird-
seed," "Pick," "Nook," "Hinky Ho," "Pickles."

Residents have no difficulty keeping up with several names
for each relative and get keen enjoyment from puzzled outsiders who try to keep identities straight. Asked her father's
name, one respondent said, "Zan Drew Huntly, but the family
called him 'Bus' and most everyone else called him 'Hunt,'
but really he went by his initials 'A. A.' " She seemed amused
when confronted with the observation that the initials didn't
fit anywhere. "Well," she explained, "his name was actually
Alexander Andrew." Here is an interesting way to view the
social system under study: "Bus" is used by the family;

---

1. This is similar to Mogey's finding that the function of surname
nicknames in rural Ireland is to distinguish subdivisions in lineage lines.
The proposition is implicit in John Mogey's *Rural Life in Northern Ireland*.

"Hunt" is used by the deme; and "A. A." is used by the outside world.

Forms of Address

Structure is also evident in the terms used for address in the valley. "Mr." and "Miss" and "Mrs." plus a person's last name are titles for addressing strangers or outsiders. Within the deme itself, first names and nicknames are used for agemates. In referring to close kin, residents employ familiar American bilateral terms, except that "mother" and "father" are sometimes "mammy" and "pappy." In addition, within the deme there is an unusual and possibly unconscious use of "aunt" and "uncle" and of "Mr." and "Miss" attached to first names. The terms "aunt" and "uncle," when used by persons other than nephews and nieces of the addressed, indicate more social distance between the speaker and person spoken to, and also far less respect than do the terms "Miss" and "Mr." preceding a first name.

To illustrate with the names "Liza Bently" and "Mont Parker": "Mrs. Bently" and "Mr. Parker" mean in effect, "You do not belong to the deme." "Liza" and "Mont" or their nicknames signify belonging, close kinship, and intimate or informal relations. "Miss Liza" and "Mr. Mont" show deep esteem and respect toward a person who is accepted as inside the social structure. But by "Aunt Liza" and "Uncle Mont" residents mean, "You're one of us, but we know your past record." The adopted aunts and uncles of the community are less likely to be participating members of the primary group.

"Miss Abbie," the respected community ideal who resides in the old homeplace, has never been referred to as "Aunt Abbie" in the writer's presence. Her sister's husband, another highly respected and accepted part of the deme, is "Mr. Jim." A number of well-known law violators are called by their first names preceded by "Uncle" and "Aunt," as are many living and dead subjects of standing derogatory jokes.

An Applecross man in an interview unintentionally pointed to the use of these terms. At one point of the conversation he said heatedly: "I ain't liking these dadburned niggers going to school with whites a bit. We need to hang them on hog killin' racks and say that will happen to them as long as they try to come into our schools. That'd stop it, wouldn't it? If one tried to come on my place, I'd shoot him." When asked later whether he would continue curing meat the way his parents said to, even if he found a way he liked better, he replied, "Yes, I wouldn't want to hurt old folks. I'm even nice to old niggers. I call them 'uncle' and 'aunt.'" In the same interview, the man used the phrase "as close as a brother" for describing a very strong affective relation.

4. The Strong Collateral Bond

EVEN more than in names and titles, the strength of the collateral bond is seen in collateral kinship relations in which warm feeling is joined with task accomplishment. One woman described the relation between her four brothers, who have adjoining farms three miles from her: "They work all day long together, eat their meals together, and then always sit around and visit with each other before they go home." One lonely wife sighed that her husband and his brothers always worked together and told each other everything.

The brother bond appears stronger than any other in the valley; moreover, love is expressed more often among siblings and cousins of both sexes than among other blood kin. One woman said that she and her three sisters "talk and cook and tell secrets and just enjoy ourselves" (some instrumental plus much affective orientation). When asked what she did with her daughters she replied, "Oh, same thing—just anything I see around their place that needs to be done" (purely instrumental). Another woman told how she was dusting tobacco and her husband was in the fields when her sister and brother-in-law came to see them. "We just stopped," she laughed, "fixed a lunch, and went fishing."

An especially co-operative and intelligent respondent gave the following relevant information in answer to how she had been spending time with her kin: "Well, my sister from Detroit was here a month ago. We had dinner, walked down to the old homeplace and got a drink out of the old spring.

33

Last Sunday after church my other sister and my brother came home with Jim and me. We talked and picked apples most of the afternoon. My cousin [also her husband's cousin] spent the day with me a few days ago. We had fun making hominy in the black lard kettle. Then my daughter spent the day with me today, and we worked like mad to get the beans picked and canned."

Similar incidents point to the purely workaday quality of relations between lineal kin as opposed to the added qualities of warmth and sociability characterizing horizontal relations.

If two persons speak warmly of each other and are not siblings or spouses, it is safe to assume that they are own cousins. "Oh, it does you good to see someone you love," said a woman while hugging her mother's brother's son. After being seriously hurt in a tractor accident, a man begged for his first cousin to be allowed in the intensive care section of the hospital. "We're like brothers," he cried. "He sold me his land. We sung and worked together since we were born. We married sisters. Let him in. He's my brother; that's all you can make of it."

Again, affect and instrumentality seem to complement each other in the strong collateral husband-wife bond. A wife confided, "I would rather give up any one of my four children than my husband." Another wife said, "We grew up together. My husband and I have never known anything else but to be together." An Applecross woman told of the death of her cousin's wife in Big Rook: "No man ever loved a woman like Jim loved his wife. If she had died two or three years sooner, Jim couldn't of stood it. But God got him ready. She was sick a long time. A week before she died he called his nine children in and sobbed, 'Mother's gonna die. You thank God he spared her to raise all nine of you. See that you hold up like men and women.' "

Yet the majority of Applecross-Millstone residents, when asked to make the choice, said they preferred a mate who was a "real help" to one who was "warm and loving." It may be that a helpful mate, like work, is considered a necessary evil in such a society. One man replied, "You need help on a place—and lovin' too, doncha?" His wife was quick to answer, "I want my same ole husband, the one I love. I don't believe in marryin' two or three times."

The Double Bond in a Bilateral System

The strong collateral bond is evident too in the expressed ideal and common occurrence of siblings marrying siblings and of siblings marrying first cousins. During the past three generations, forty-two cases of multiple marriages within sibling groups appear in the genealogies of thirty couples (approximately three hundred marriages), and a number of these are triple marriages. A mother sighed, "My three daughters married Ed's three sons; ain't nothin' that brings a family together like that." There are also two cases of the sororate, or the marriage of one man with two or more sisters. For every case in the genealogies of siblings marrying siblings, diagrammed as

$$\overline{\underset{O \,=\, \Delta}{\overline{}}\;\underset{O \,=\, \Delta}{}}$$

there are at least two cases of siblings marrying first cousins, diagrammed as

$$\underset{O \,=\, \Delta}{\overset{\Delta}{}}\quad\underset{O \,=\, \Delta}{\overset{}{}}\;\overset{O}{}$$

Before going into how marriage choice is affected by collateral ties, let us illustrate some consequences of such unions.

Female respondent A of Applecross and female respondent B of Millstone expressed mutual preferences for each other in their sociometric choices. "We're together every day," they said; "Oh, we love each other." The women are first cousins, since A's mother and B's father are siblings. They are second cousins, as A's father and B's mother are first cousins. Furthermore, A and B themselves married brothers. The diagram looks like this:

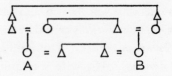

FIG. 8—*Double cousins who married brothers.*

In another case, a woman X said she thought "a great deal" of the man Y. Their mothers are sisters, their grandfathers are brothers, and they married first cousins. Their diagram is as follows:

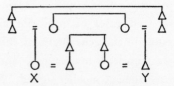

FIG. 9—*Double cousins who married cousins.*

As pointed out in the discussion of cousin marriages, the particular mate selections of X and Y function to maintain a sibling-like relation, rather than a marital one, between these own cousins. Either bond—marital or that similar to the sibling—is an expression of a close collateral tie, the latter appearing to be a conservative alternative to the former where marriage would be with one closer than a single-bond first cousin. A variation of the expression of this tie occurred in a church service recently, in which four first cousins from three sibling groups stood together at the altar and took membership vows. Their coming forward was a surprise to their parents, none of whom were present at the service. "We just wanted to come up together," they explained. Still another variation occurred in the marriage of distant cousins who grew up as brother and sister, being reared by the same couple.

A very close relation holds between two men E and G, who understand and are proud of their connections. G's grandmother and E's mother are sisters. E's father and G's grandfathers on both sides are brothers. The two men not only are first cousins once removed through the first relation but they are double first cousins once removed through the second.

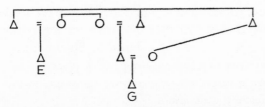

FIG. 10—*A first- and double-first-cousin relation.*

A Millstone girl, "Ego," asked what her relation is to the children born of the union between her father's niece and her mother's nephew. This is a double relationship, since the children's parents are both Ego's first cousins, but it is not a double-first-cousin-once-removed relation.

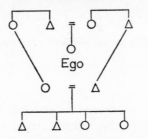

FIG. 11—*An unnamed double relation.*

It is clear that the most meaningful ties are those collateral ones which involve both parents, the two basic ones being siblings and double cousins. In a deme, however, there are meaningful double bonds other than these. For example, G in Figure 10 is very attached to his mother's father, who is also his father's uncle. The double bond, as we have defined and described it here, is the tie of greatest conceivable value in a bilateral system.

The Collateral Bond and Mate Selection

Rather than following a consistent giving and receiving of spouses between particular family lines, multiple marriages within sibling groups present definite patterns which take form and break up over several generations. Given bilateral reckoning, cousin marriage preference, and the tendency for sibs to stand united in marriage choice, such patterns as those illustrated below result. As shown in Figure 12, triple marriages between two sibling groups took place for two generations with a single marriage setting the stage, so to speak, in each preceding generation.

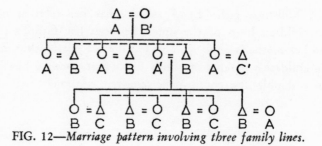

FIG. 12—*Marriage pattern involving three family lines.*

Taking A′ as our reference: A′ and her two sisters married three brothers bearing her mother's maiden name. Three children of A′ also married three siblings bearing the married name of another sister to A′. Thus the kin of B′ became marriageable to A′ and her sibs, and the kin of C′ became marriageable to her offspring.

The second diagram is one that involves five family lines (A, B, C, D, and E). In the third generation, six As married Bs, two Cs married Bs, and one B married a B. In the fourth generation five Cs married Bs, one C married an A, and one A married a B. Notice how sibling groups are closely involved in the third and fourth lines and how the offspring of

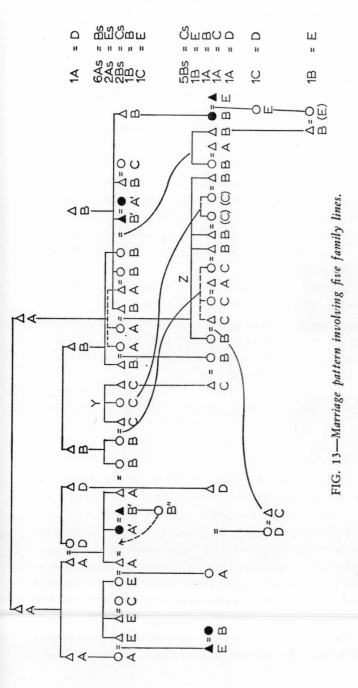

FIG. 13—Marriage pattern involving five family lines.

Note: Four sets of couples are shaded to show duplication—the A'=B' couple in the third line and the E=B couple at each end of the fourth line. Parentheses around a letter indicate that the given letter stands for the mother's maiden name.

the sibling group Y (who are first cousins) claimed spouses from the sibling group Z plus a first cousin of the Z group.

The important thing seen here and throughout genealogies for the area is how multiple marriages reveal siblings and first cousins standing together in their choices of sibling groups. The trend may even explain one of the few divorces in the area. On the third generation line there are two sets of spouses that have been shaded to indicate duplication. According to residents, A' took B' away from his first wife. One might suppose that with no unmarried choices left A' did not feel as constrained by the deme's strict sex norms as she felt compelled to have a spouse of the model description— one in the family line into which her siblings and cousins were currently marrying.

It can be seen in Figure 13 that A' has a brother who married her husband's daughter, B''. This same thing recently happened again. That is, a woman's brother married her husband's daughter by a previous union. In the second case (diagrammed below) the woman and her sister are married to their first cousins, who are brothers.

A similar explanation could be given for the union, not shown in the diagram, of a young man to a much older woman. The older woman, once widowed, belongs to a family line which for three generations has been supplying most of the mates for another family with which the young man strongly verbally identifies himself. Could the compulsion to fit into his "adopted" family's marriage structure have been a major factor in the young man's decision to marry the widow, almost thirty years his senior?

In view of the factors in our deme which appear to play a part in marriage patterns, it is reasonable to assign primary strength to the unity of the sibling group, especially since that unity is so evident in work relations, residence, and other interaction processes. A popular approach to social structure is to consider it, not as a force exerting pressure on individuals through jural rules, but as the unintended consequence of many individual choices. This approach may be useful in understanding such practices as the sororate and close-cousin marriages, which are optional and permitted rather than obligatory. Sometimes, however, individual motivation appears to be overcome by factors which are clearly exigencies of a given social structure. Consider a final case.

A young man was accidentally killed by one of his own buddies in the Korean War. In accord with the close expressive relation between husbands and wives in the area, his wife's grief was in much evidence, and she vowed she would never marry again. Her deceased husband's first cousin was with him when the accident occurred. At first she welcomed the cousin's visits to get details of her husband's death, but when she realized the cousin was in love with her she stopped seeing him. She had known his mother all her life, was some kin to her, and called her "aunt." Not wanting to hurt the older woman's feelings, she accepted "aunt's" invitations, and the young man in this way continued his courtship to the point of marriage. The girl's initial decision to remain a widow was a part of the strong collateral husband-wife bond, and the suitor's calling card was a part of the strong collateral first-cousin bond. The combined effects of distance from sibship, propinquity, and quality of interaction apparently exerted their pressure in the young man's favor.

Part II. COMMUNITY

5. Territorial References

COMMUNITY planners today emphasize the ways in which social relations may be shaped by physical characteristics. One of the first things one notices about Turnabout Hollow is its banana shape, contrasted to the oval shape of Applecross-Millstone. Applecross and Millstone together cover about five square miles or three thousand acres, comprising a total of thirty-three farms. Applecross contains twenty-five and Millstone eight farm households. Turnabout Hollow covers about three square miles and contains thirty-one farm households. Turnabout Hollow, as a physical area, is harder to identify. Its boundaries are familial rather than

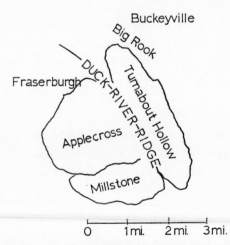

FIG. 14—*Shapes of the Applecross, Millstone, and Turnabout Hollow Valleys.*

territorial. Applecross and Millstone are described as extending "to the bridge" or "to Slide Hill," but Turnabout Hollow extends to "where A family lives" in one direction and B family in another.

As stated earlier, Duck River Ridge is the boundary between Turnabout Hollow and Applecross-Millstone. Along the Ridge there are coves, of which Turnabout Hollow, being long and narrow, has a larger proportion. Domestic households tend to segregate in these coves with new family units settling near the husband's parents. In Turnabout coves are six cases of parents and married children living in adjacent houses, five of these being married sons. Patrilocal residence is also involved in one of the two cases of married children living in the same house with Turnabout Hollow parents. All Applecross-Millstone homes are presently single-family dwellings. The only case of parental-local residence in Applecross-Millstone involves a brother and sister who live near each other at the lower foot of the Ridge and who both have married daughters nearby, but the homes of the daughters (first cousins) are actually closer together than the parent-child residences.

The spatial aspect having theoretical import is that, by residence and physical description, Turnabout Hollow, unlike Applecross-Millstone, is more a set of corporate families than part of a corporate community.

Territory and Occupation

Stronger lineal ties in Turnabout Hollow are seen not only in residence patterns but also in work activities. With the exception of one widow whose son-in-law lives near and works her place, Applecross-Millstone work-teams are organized collaterally along brother and cousin and neighbor relations. By contrast, in Turnabout Hollow several father-son teams farm together; one son-in-law works for the public and furnishes equipment while his father-in-law does the labor on both men's farms; one father and son paint signboards for the same company, and a second son plans to move back to the hollow from Detroit to work with them; another father and son spread lime fertilizer together; and a nephew works adjoining land that belongs to his aunt who has no sons.

If one judges on the basis of whether daily activities of the residents are carried on within the area itself, Turnabout Hollow does not meet the requirements of "community" as well as Applecross-Millstone. Places of residence, of work, and of all other social relations coincide more closely for Applecross-Millstone families than for Turnabout families.

A third of the men in Turnabout Hollow and a fourth of the women work outside the community. Turnabout Hollow farms average only about sixty acres and are not very uniform in size, some having as few as twenty acres. Applecross-Millstone farms average ninety acres and are quite uniform in size. All Applecross-Millstone families are full-time farmers, with the men doing some local carpentering, trucking, and trading, and the women filling some part-time roles of seamstress or paper hanger. One man and two women in Applecross have factory jobs outside the community. Neighbors say that the man is trying to do too much, and they ask the women how long it will be before they can quit work. The man and one of the women are considering moving.

There are six Turnabout Hollow tenants. Four of the landlords are absentee owners and two live in Turnabout Hollow. Two additional pieces of land in Turnabout Hollow are worked by men who live elsewhere. No Applecross-Millstone land is worked by outsiders, but there is one absentee owner of land in Applecross-Millstone. He and his wife (third cousins to each other) both grew up in Applecross and now live ten miles away. He could hardly be called absentee, since he is in the valley daily, working with the men who live on his three farms. Two of the men are close kin to him, and the third has lived on his place more than thirty years. All three men have been told they can stay on the farms until they die. The agreement is being borne out by one who continues to reside on the farm although he has a paralyzed wife and is unable to work himself.

Contrasting the territorial aspects of work for Applecross-Millstone and Turnabout Hollow, then, we find that Applecross-Millstone has more occupational homogeneity, more collateral work arrangements (as against Turnabout Hollow's lineal teams), and less contact with the outside world.

Community Centers

The country store sits at the center of Applecross-Millstone life. It opens at 6:00 a.m., closes around 9:00 p.m. except on Friday and Saturday nights when the last families usually leave around midnight. It is a meeting place for young and old of both sexes, a news center, an every-evening social gathering place. Families have the habit of visiting at the store after supper and during slack work days. Men regularly eat one large can of pork and beans and one fried pie on the porch steps during rushed seasons. The storekeeper is quick to open a loaf of bread and hand out salt and pepper.

If one asks the whereabouts of kinsfolk, the answer is, "If you go to the store, you're shore to catch some of them." The men gather around the wood stove in the back of the store by winter or on the porch and in the crossroads by summer, while the women sit at the front of the store the year around. Messages and articles and children are left and picked up at the store. Individual dates and groups of young people meet there. Children are sent on errands to and from the store, being told, "You're still in your first legs." [1]

During the course of a Friday evening at the store, one

---

1. After sending his son on an errand, one father confided, "When I was a boy, I used to wonder when I'd get my second pair of legs."

is likely to hear some animal talk from the men as they squat on the porch or support themselves with first one hip and then the opposite foot pressed flat against one of the porch pillars:

Did you know crocodiles cry all the time? Yeller stuff runs out o' their eyes and mouth and draws flies. When their mouth gets full o' flies, Clap! . . . Well, did you ever hear tell of a hoop snake? It can ketch itself into a hoop and roll downhill. It has a barb that sticks out when it rolls, and if that barb hits a tree, the tree'll die.

Talk may turn to the decision of who is the ugliest man in the community or who has had the most trouble lately. Big Rook incidents inevitably follow:

You 'member when those men shot through Aunt Lila's house? Why, she got her gun, shot one man between the eyes dead center, emptied her gun on the others, reloaded and emptied again, reloaded and emptied again, till every man was out of sight.

Talk usually ends on a mutual congratulatory note regarding residents' choice of a home:

My cousin has been to country where houses weren't no bigger than this porch. You could see right through 'em. Every house had an ole cow stake-roped to the front, to a little patch o' grass here and a little patch there. I never seen cows stake-roped. Brother, that's pore! Where you see black locust an' blue grass like here, it's good country.

The men follow the same pattern Saturday nights. Several lie down with only their head and neck upright against the porch wall:

What's wrong with the world is folks got too much cow's milk in their blood these days. A hundred more years and we'll all be like Cain's race—horns on our haids, eight-feet tall, all misshaped. Cain's wife was a animal. . . . Did you know elephants carry their young two years, and alligators and turtles turn over on their backs to mate? . . .

John took his wife to Vandy[2] to git a tumor out. That Vandy doctor told John she'd have to stay a week and he'd have to go home. John looked at him and says, "I got me a little doctor I know that will tend to that and send her home and let me sleep with her." He did, and John slept with her that night. She's doin' real good too. . . .

I hear Jack jest walked out of court. Course, they give 'im 'leven months and twenty-nine days for shootin' his boy, but he's never served a hour, and never will. . . . Big Rook's gettin thicker an' meaner all the time. I used to live there— killin's every week, but friendly folks. . . . Did you ever go by the old house where that nigger baby was powsoned? Day or night you hear it cry, and you hear a creakin' like someone rockin' in a straight chair. . . .

You know, this is the best place in all the world fer mindin' your own business. But you go over that hill yonder, and it's like goin' to Europe. . . . And the niggers had another mournin' all night last night over on the highway. By the time they git through dancin' and yellin,' that daid nigger will stink.

Women's store talk revolves more around kin news:

Have you seen Della's baby's picture frame? I wish I had one jest like it for my sister's baby that was born daid.

The frame mentioned contains a lock of Della's dead baby's hair, a baby spoon, a bow off one of the funeral sprays, and some lace from one of the baby's dresses, sewed onto a magaine picture of a small child. The ladies continue:

Last night my girl said, "Mother, you're looking more and more like Grandmother." And my husband said, "Yeah, and if she gets to lookin' any more like her, I'll leave."

There is some laughter from the group at this, but they look solemn during the next comments:

Did you know Bill won't let his wife's mother cross the

2. Vanderbilt Hospital in Nashville.

Ridge? . . . Well, I heard Sue Huntly's husband—over at
Big Rook—walked out on her. They say he left his false
teeth, his eye glasses and watch, and a note on the dresser
saying, "If I stay, I'll kill you." And no one's saw him since.
. . . Fureigner, he was! Likely won't ever be back. Do you
have some cannin' jars I could use? I'd be much obliged. . . .

Sally, I'll be over in the mornin' to give you a permanent, if
I feel well enough in the haid. Haven't felt good in the haid
lately. . . . You mean Monday. I'm not goin' to preachin'
tomorrow if the men ain't cut down them growed-up bushes
'round the church. . . . I see Tom's ready to go. We aim to
stop by Sis and Bud's 'fore dark. Bud ain't burnt ten gallons
of gas in his ole Kaiser since the boy kilt hisself five years ago.

Besides meeting at Applecross Store, more than 70 percent of Applecross-Millstone residents gather regularly at
Applecross Baptist and Methodist churches. Four couples attend a nearby Presbyterian church, two women a nearby
Church of Christ, and seven men seldom attend any church.
Since the closing of the Millstone School fifteen years ago,
all Applecross-Millstone children are sent to school at Fraserburgh, two miles west of Applecross. In a very real sense, all
families "belong to" Applecross Store and to their churches,
and to these institutions alone. No Applecross-Millstone parent
is a member of the Fraserburgh Parent-Teacher Association.
Without exception, no Applecross-Millstone adult is a member of any formal organization other than the church.

These aspects of community cohesion are missing for Turnabout Hollow. In contrast to the unanimous nonmembership
status of Applecross-Millstone adults (except for local church
affiliations), a third of the Turnabout adults are active in the
Parent-Teacher Association, Demonstration Club, Eastern
Star, Lions Club, or Masons, all of which meet outside Turnabout Hollow itself. Four Turnabout families cross the Ridge
to attend the Methodist church at Applecross and one to attend the Baptist. Six go to Salt Lick Cumberland Presbyterian

Church and four to Harpeth Church of Christ, both located in the southwest end of Turnabout Hollow. Five attend churches in other communities; one even attends in Nashville. More than half of Turnabout residents do not go to any church regularly; those who do tend to congregate as close kin groups.

Peddlers are another dividing element in Turnabout Hollow. A few families buy weekly supplies at Applecross and Groundhog Creek stores below the Ridge, and a few at Buckeyville above the Ridge, where they have kin; but Turnabout residents buy mainly from a traveling store, an old school bus grocery and general store that comes weekly from a town eight miles northeast. There is a good road through Turnabout Hollow, and it is included in this and other peddlers' routes. At the scheduled hour, residents can be seen waiting at the road for the traveling store man, who is a kinsman himself. Younger lineal relatives often wait with older kin and carry heavy supplies back into the hollows for them.

School attendance is an additional dividing factor. Children in the northwest half of Turnabout Hollow attend school at Fraserburgh. Children from the southeast end go to Groundhog Creek School, the adjoining community three miles south, and to a high school in a village of about four hundred persons, four miles east. The old Hawk Hill schoolhouse, located in Turnabout Hollow, has been a Negro church for the last fifteen years. The church is considered an alien and unnatural group from "over the highway." Weird stories are told by Turnabout families about all-night mournings for the dead and mysterious and mystic practices of the Negro congregation. No Negroes live in Turnabout Hollow or in Applecross-Millstone, and feelings against them are exceedingly strong. Unlike Hawk Hill, the old Millstone schoolhouse is shared by neighbors for storing hay; its use by outsiders would probably not be tolerated, especially if the outsiders were Negroes.

Upper and Lower Ridge Differences

Structural differences already given in this section may be summarized as follows: Though the sibling bond is strong in both areas, social structure in Turnabout Hollow has far more lineal emphases than it does in Applecross-Millstone where collateral relationships predominate. This means that in residence and work and visitation patterns, the parent-child bond is stronger in Turnabout Hollow; but in Applecross-Millstone cohesion is maintained more through neighbor (territorial), cousin, and sibling interaction. Applecross-Millstone families all patronize Applecross Store, and all the children attend school at Fraserburgh. Families in Turnabout Hollow are divided in the stores they use and the schools their children attend. They not only are more divided in the churches they attend than are Applecross-Millstone families, but a fourth fewer of them go to any church. No Applecross-Millstone adults belong to any organization other than the church; a third of Turnabout adults are members of diverse groups that meet in neighboring communities. Also, more of the daily work activity of Turnabout residents takes place outside the community.

There are other differences between Turnabout Hollow and Applecross-Millstone that are important to our analysis. One concerns education. Only one person in Applecross-Millstone reported that she had finished high school. This woman grew up in an orphans' home, though her family is in Big Rook; she is one of two women from "outside" the community. Five Applecross-Millstone residents dropped out of high school in their senior year. The majority of adults finished the sixth grade. In Turnabout Hollow, education ranges widely from no schooling to a college degree. Many Turnabout adults plan for their children to finish high school and get a few years of college. This ambition is not shared by Applecross-Millstone residents, who say, referring to one well-educated Turnabout woman, "Since she went to college, she's taken charge of her husband."

A second important difference is that, with the exception of two women, Applecross-Millstone families are lifelong residents of the valley. A third of the families in Turnabout Hollow are not. A number of former Applecross persons who married "strangers" now live in Turnabout Hollow. Several Big Rook families have moved eastward to Turnabout Hollow. One couple who were absentee owners of Turnabout Hollow land for forty years have recently returned and built an expensive home; the man quickly assumed a leadership position.

A third difference has to do with material possessions. Some houses and furnishings in Turnabout Hollow look much finer and some much poorer than do the more uniform Applecross-Millstone homes. Also noticeable are the thoroughbred animals in Turnabout Hollow, whereas Applecross-Millstone families own only mixed breeds. In Turnabout Hollow possessions and animals are more often "shown off," and there is more talk of personal achievement. In Applecross-Millstone anyone who brags is liable to harsh teasing.

In other words, there is more status differentiation in Turnabout Hollow as seen in differences in amount of land and equipment, number and type of cattle, kind of house, years of formal education. Individual family ambition is more evident there than in Applecross-Millstone. As will be discussed in Chapter VI, leaders are also evident in Turnabout Hollow but not in Applecross-Millstone.

The eighth chapter of this book deals with an even more striking difference between these two areas. In Turnabout Hollow and nearby upper-Ridge territory we find a present pattern and a long history of violence that is not found in Applecross-Millstone and surrounding lower-Ridge communities. Since the consideration of violence may be aided by an historical analysis of the important physical boundary, Duck River Ridge, the discussion of that boundary will be reserved for the chapter dealing with strain.

Boundary Maintenance: Endogamy and Migration

External boundaries around the Ridge are not easily penetrated. The practice of valley persons of not marrying "strangers" constitutes the most important means of holding boundaries tight. These are highly stable, intermarrying residential groups that have persisted for five or six generations.

The stability and endogamy of the community are seen in the genealogies themselves and in a comparison of names supplied by couples interviewed with names on the original census forms from the 1850 first individual count through the 1880 release. In the districts involved no family name appears on these census sheets which is not also in the writer's genealogies, and approximately two-thirds of the given names in the 1850–1880 census records are in the genealogies. Residing with the forty-eight couples of 1880, direct ancestors of the population studied, were the following relatives, who can also be identified genealogically: three of the wives' sisters and two of the husbands' sisters, a husband's brother, a husband's parents, a wife's mother, two uncles, an aunt, two nieces, a nephew, a son-in-law, a daughter-in-law, plus one unidentified schoolteacher.

Other support of the community's stability and endogamy lies in the following data. Of the 62 adults questioned in Applecross-Millstone, only two grew up more than 10 miles away from their present home, and five have never lived in any other house. Only four of the 62 persons lived more than 10 miles away at the time they married. The majority of the couples have known each other "always" and lived less than three miles from one another before marriage. For the 30 Applecross-Millstone couples, the table shows the distances mates lived apart before marriage.

TABLE 2

Distances Between Residences Before Marriage

Traveling Miles From Each Other	Number of Couples
0-4	19
5-9	8
10-15	3
More than 15	0

There is a significant sex difference in responses to these questions. The man consistently reported he had lived closer to his spouse and had known his spouse longer before marriage. Some of the discrepancy between couples' reports on the length of time they had known each other before marriage lies in the fact that marriage age for men exceeds that for women by six years. The variation in age and memory span does not account for all the difference, however. One husband said he had known his wife "always," and the wife said she had known him "a couple of years" before marriage, but she added, "I had seen him around, of course." Another husband said he lived in "walking distance" of his wife before marriage, and she said they lived "550 miles apart." The matter resolved itself when the couple explained they both had gone to Detroit to work and live with relatives, who were Applecross migrants living in the same Detroit neighborhood.

Migration practices are important in the perpetuation of valley structure. There are two ways in which residents guard against a population threat that would upset their present system of adapting environing conditions to attain their goals. The line is held against outsiders by marriage and property rules, but also the natural increase must be dealt with, since it could give imbalance to the economic structure by decreasing the size of farms. The average completed Applecross-

Millstone nuclear family is only 4.7 members. Four of the thirteen women past child-bearing age have only one child, and there are just three women who have five or more. Considering the natural increase alone, a minimum amount of emigration is needed to maintain a stationary population.

Allowance, however, must be made for the individuals who do not sufficiently internalize or follow valley norms to remain there. A kind of self-banishment from the area is common after family estrangements or after love loss or property loss. This is what residents mean when they say, "He [or she] ain't been back since." The self-banishment may be permanent, as in suicide cases such as committed by a girl who had separated herself from the deme by her choice of a college education or as committed by a man who shot himself after shooting his former wife. Also, the self-banishment may involve moving completely away or just moving to an acceptable "extension" (see paragraphs to follow), from which one's children might some day return to the valley. There is no problem in making up for population loss below the Ridge, for spouses can always be secured from above the Ridge, where family fertility is higher. One upper-Ridge woman who married a Millstone man and now lives in Millstone, said she was one of thirty-two children, all born of the same parents. Of upper-Ridge families, many of whom are engaged in moonshining, it is said, "They make lots of corn and have a heap of children." It is significant that the population problem is the one world-wide problem that seems to worry these people, and they speak of it often and fearfully.

As the Southern Appalachian study reports, migration involves more than persons moving from one surface of the land to another; migrants feel more secure about leaving an area and are more easily integrated at the receiving end of the migration stream when they are able to join family members who have moved out before them.[3] Three extensions of the Ridge community were located.

One of the extensions is in Brechin, fifteen miles northeast of Turnabout Hollow. There Huntlys bought cheap land many years ago and started in the lumbering business. One Brechin resident explained: "This was Miller Holler when we moved in, but there ain't but two Millers left. We call it Huntly Holler now." There have been eight new Huntly houses built in Brechin in the last five years. One ninety-year-old man complained, "If the world stands another hundred years, this'll be as thick as Columbia through here." Then he asked in wonderment: "Did you ever look at the babies in the county hospital? They're as thick as chicks in an electric chicken hatch." Within sight of the man's home, one can count seven separate farm houses belonging to his brother, his sister, his sister's son, two of his sister's sons' daughters, his own daughter, and his daughter's son. Another daughter lives two miles away. A man from Big Rook recently went bond for a brother's son, who lives several miles away, when the boy got in legal trouble. Moving from Turnabout Hollow, these families talk and act like Turnabout people, and they have the same residence and work patterns. One Turnabout woman said she and her neighbors were often mistaken for Brechin residents by strangers, who commented, "You just act like them," or "You talk like them." Even epidemics, such as the 1957 hepatitis one, have a way of appearing simultaneously in the two communities.

There is a neighborhood in the county seat of Kinbrace County that is composed of six or seven families who have moved from the Ridge community. Two of these moved after they were closely involved in a triple killing in Turnabout Hollow thirty years ago. A retired Methodist minister

3. Thomas R. Ford (ed.), *The Southern Appalachian Region: A Survey*, p. 76.

from Applecross is at the center of the county-seat neighborhood. A daughter and a granddaughter of two of the county-seat families have recently married back into Turnabout Hollow and reside there.

A third extension of these valleys is in Detroit, Michigan, where brothers and cousins since depression years have been going together to find work. One informant, at eighteen, and his eight cousins left Applecross and became employed in a box factory in Detroit. He is back in Applecross today, but his son has gone to Detroit to work in a brewery; the son was persuaded by two of his cousins who have jobs selling cigarettes there. A girl who went to Detroit to visit her sister married her sister's husband's brother while there. Mention has already been made of the young man and woman from the valley who went to Detroit to live with relatives, courted and married in Detroit, and returned to the valley to live.

Moving to join family lines in Brechin or the county seat or in Detroit 550 miles away does not separate a person from valley connections as cleanly as moving to Nashville or even to some nearby farm communities. Family lines and attitudes seem to be largely maintained in the county-seat, Brechin, and Detroit extensions—so much so that these persons are permitted to move back to their valley homes or to marry back into valley farms. For a way of life to be continued, a migration stream rather than individual migrations is required; the streams have been small but they have been steady. As far as the study reveals, these are the only "acceptable" places for one to move. Moving elsewhere necessitates a break in marriage alliances and socially alienates persons from the deme.

With such family lines and dominant kinship patterns extended to rural nonfarm, county seat, and urban areas, one could profitably view theories of the metropolitan area's exerting dominance from the other end of the line. Not only does the city exert a wide influence on outlying families and neighborhoods with its occupational structure; it is also affected by the ascriptive emphases of various kinship and ethnic structures. These are rooted in, and maintain connections with, rural farm communities and exert attitudinal and organizational influences into rural nonfarm, town, and metropolitan centers.

6. Work Norms and Practices

FARMING is the main occupation of the Ridge communities. Cash income is from the sale of approximately two acres of tobacco, the beef and milk from about a dozen cows, and whiskey. Since most valley families care less for the flavor of beef, cows are strictly cash stock, and goats and pigs are raised for family consumption. Corn is not carried to market, but enough is grown for feeding hogs, chickens, mules, and for the whiskey operations.

Women and children stay busy during blackberry season, gathering and preserving; berries are the favorite fruit. Family gardens provide a wide variety of fresh vegetables to be canned for home use. Valley families prefer the taste of vegetables steam-canned in quart jars, though a few have bought deepfreezes. After the men have done the initial plowing for the family gardens they turn the work over to their wives.

In Applecross-Millstone 92 percent of the couples have segregated work roles; that is, husbands and wives do most of the household chores independently. When asked whether the husband or wife did "all" or just "more" of six selected family jobs (see question 44 of the questionnaire), 35 percent reported all roles segregated, 22 percent reported five segregated and one joint role, 35 percent reported four segregated and two joint roles, and 8 percent reported three of each role type. No couple reported doing more than half the chores jointly. Moreover, much segregation was reported within work labeled "joint." In the activity most often viewed as joint—repairing things around the house—several couples explained that the man carpenters and the woman paints. Likewise, the man pays the bills and the wife keeps the books. In gardening, the man plows and the woman hoes and gathers. In general, women care for the smaller farm animals and men care for machinery and the larger animals.

Mules and tractors are used equally for farm work. On the narrow, steep strips which must be cultivated, mules and a hillside plow are more practical than a tractor. Farmers have inheritances of mule-drawn equipment, the know-how and habits for farming with mules, and there is more pride of ownership in a good team of mules than in a tractor. Fancy harnesses with red tassels and polished brass hame knobs are sometimes seen. Teams trained to pull timber in Kinbrace County hill country often compete with other teams from Tennessee and Kentucky at county and state fair mule-pullings. Neighbors show special interest in a man's mules that have competed in weight-dragging contests.

Burley tobacco is ahead of all other legally marketable crops as cash income. Only a small amount is used locally by men who whittle their own hickory bowl pipes and smoke or chew twists of their own tobacco. Tobacco, like cotton, requires much hand labor and has certain urgent seasons. Tobacco crops in the valley are handled by "swapping out," that is, by neighbor work-teams who carry out the seasonal activities first at one team member's farm and then at another's.

Male work-teams prepare the tobacco seedbeds early each spring and keep weeds and insects poisoned. Poisoning within the seedbeds is done by outlining the beds with logs, covering them with plastic or cheesecloth, and pumping gas into them. Covers are tied to the log frames to protect the tobacco from frost, insects, and from blowing weed seeds. Each farmer fertilizes, plows, and harrows his own field in preparation for the young tobacco plants. Late in May work-teams pull the plants out of the seedbeds and set them in the fields. When setting is done by hand it is called "pegging" and engages men, women, and children. If the ground is dry enough, two men plus a driver of a simple machine drawn by mule or tractor set the tobacco. The machine opens the furrows, waters the plants that the two men place by hand, and covers them.

Individual families kill the harmful insects on their tobacco plants by sprinkling poison through a can attached to a stick. Wives "poison the tobacco" until it gets waist high, but it is the husbands' part to poison insects on the taller tobacco and keep the fields plowed. As the tobacco heads, seeds are topped and thrown aside to help the plants spread. Toward late summer the leaves begin to dry. Work-teams again make the rounds to cut and hang the tobacco in high-roofed barns. Burley tobacco doesn't have to be fired. Through the Christmas season, work-teams strip it and then take it to the county-seat warehouse to be auctioned. Each farmer remains at the warehouse, watching his tobacco until the auctioneer and buyers come by and it is sold. This is the farmer's main annual cash income. It is supplemented during the year by the selling of milk and calves.

The above description is more typical of Applecross-Millstone than of Turnabout Hollow. Land above the Ridge is less fertile, and more cattle are seen there than below. Also, moonshining is big business above the Ridge, and tobacco is of less importance.

Swapping Out

It is essential to understand some of the differences in work activities and norms above and below the Ridge. In Applecross-Millstone three to five (in most cases, four) men form a work-team; these are close neighbors who are usually either brothers or cousins. Some of the teams have been swapping out for more than thirty years. The men say there are no leaders of their teams, and apparently they are accurately describing their system. When a farmer is ready for help he is expected to visit the members of his team after supper the evening before and ask for their help. On his own farm, a man may give directions such as where to plant the tobacco or where to hang it. If two men ask for help at the same time, the group decides which is "hurting worse" and helps that man first. If a member of the team does not show up to help, then when he asks for help on his own farm the other team members say, "We didn't see you working at our place last week."

The practice of reciprocating is so well understood in Applecross-Millstone that residents never mind asking for help. In fact, the failure to ask for help when help is needed is condemned by lower-Ridge kinsfolk. This manner of expression is evident in other relations too. For example, in speaking of ones in the community dear to them, persons more commonly say, "Oh, how he loves me," than "Oh, how I love him." To say "he loves me" implies "I love him."

The rule of returning in kind also extends to those outside the deme. The writer left a pie at the widower's house. Half a year passed and he did not mention it. Then one Sunday he walked to church with a load of sweetcorn in his arms and "thank you" written all over his face: "Hard to get a stand this year in the garden. Ain't furgot that pecan pie." Another man gave the writer's family a claw-hammer handle which he had carved beautifully out of white hickory in appreciation for a hand tool the family had given him. A complete hog jaw, hickory smoked, was offered to the writer's sons after they volunteered help in handpegging tobacco. Hardly a Sunday passed during the two-year valley pastorate without gifts of bacon, fish, goat meat, lard, fresh and canned vegetables, and fruit. And always followed: "You give us spiritual food, preacher, and we'll give you physical."

The strong norm of reciprocity below the Ridge saves face for the farmer, because asking for help and returning help are expected. This is not the case above the Ridge, where a person often curses his neighbor for not helping him but will not ask for help. Turnabout Hollow residents verbalize the helping norm more strongly than do their lower-Ridge neighbors. "You ought to help *before* you're asked to," they say emphatically, but there is far less "helping" there.

Work-teams are less common above the Ridge. A Big Rook man explained, "By the time you round them up and feed them it's cheaper and easier just to hire." Above the Ridge, where family fertility is higher, children and women often do rougher labor along with the men. Sex-role segregation is not nearly as strict in Turnabout Hollow as in Applecross-Millstone. One Applecross man told of how he went back to his house after a Big Rook woman joined a group of workers in the corn field. "She could pull more corn than most men," he said, "but I wasn't going to pull corn with her." The same man would be teased if he pulled slips (young tobacco plants for transplanting), as this is considered women's and children's work below the Ridge, but he would think nothing of stripping tobacco with a woman.

Applecross-Millstone farmers say that swapping out is "the only way to do it. If you hire, all you can hire is young boys, old men, and niggers." They also explain how seasons have "moved" through the past years so that a man "needs a ready team because he doesn't have as long nowadays to get in a crop." This is not only their explanation of work-teams but their justification of the tractor and other mechanization.

Though swapping out has some advantages, it probably is not so much an economic necessity as an overwhelming choice below the Ridge. Among its advantages is that the men who work together year after year understand one another, each knowing what the other likes, is willing to do, and how he wants things done: "Every man knows jest what to do. We jest zip along—kill hogs, haul hay, tobacco. We don't count hours." One man who is teased by the whole community for his shirking is expected to pull a few slips, then go to the house and talk with the women. Since the man's wife is "the best cook in the country," however, the others in his work-team continue to accept him.

Another advantage of swapping out is that equipment can be shared as well as manpower. A resident explained that for years he had furnished two mules and his neighbor two unmarried grown sons in their arrangement. "When I need the boys I holler. When they need the mules they come to the top of the Ridge and call down. I brought them up to that. They done it all their lives." The practice of bartering rather than buying is an advantage to farmers who do not have much excess cash. One farmer said that otherwise it would take him ninety dollars just to get his tobacco set out; he was figuring three men a day for three days.

A further advantage is that swapping out eliminates the necessity of having "rank strangers" penetrating valley boundaries. Residents are especially wary of visits from "candy-dates" and of government interference with agricultural activities. An Applecross man became extremely angry when the agricultural census was taken: "They got their fingers in yore nose," he complained with much cursing.

That swapping out in Applecross-Millstone goes deeper than just expediency is shown in answers on the formal questionnaire. When asked whether they would prefer working with a man they knew well or a stranger who was more efficient and faster, only one Applecross-Millstone man chose the stranger. The exception, who in practice works daily with his brother across the road, had moved to the edge of Applecross from Buckeyville above the Ridge. Typical responses for worker preferences were:

I'd rather have someone I knowd well and that way and could get along with.

You take a stranger. You don't know much about him.

On a farm it's different from public work. A stranger could lose you more than he makes you in cutting tobacco. I want someone close who knows my place—not someone just interested in money from a day's work.

I'd rather have an old man I know that has to stop and rest.

I want a good neighbor to work with.

A fast man's no good on a farm. I want a neighbor that's slow and sure.

I want someone I know and can trust.

I don't want no cocky stranger working with me and telling me what to do.

Swapping out is very often verbally identified with good neighbor relations. One elderly man, when asked, "Do you swap out work?" answered:

Oh yes, I have *very* good neighbors—never had no trouble with them—wouldn't live in a community where I couldn't have neighbors. Take anything—if you don't stick together you can't do anything. Have to get in the union. I get along with all my neighbors. We cut tops, haul hay, everything. I haven't got an enemy. I can get along with anybody if they do half way right. I never have been arrested even.

As the man talked, he paused each time a neighbor passed his window, and he would not resume conversation until the neighbor was completely out of sight. He usually identified the neighbor and the neighbor's mission aloud. Once when he was in doubt he called to his wife, "Where's Tom going, reckon?"

Moonshining

Neighbors and social relations with community members constitute a long-standing economic arrangement in Apple-cross-Millstone, but as was pointed out in the section on territoriality, arrangements in Turnabout Hollow are more familial. Joint-role relations are more common in Turnabout Hollow; and a larger nuclear family, rather than male neighbors, more often share field and other work. The raising of corn and cattle in Turnabout Hollow does not seem as conducive to swapping-out practices. And unlicensed stills, far more prevalent above the Ridge, are usually long-standing family arrangements. It is desirable to have a still in the same family and location over a period of years so that buyers and haulers know the layout. Since still operation is illegal, strict secrecy must be observed with persons other than the selected personnel. In the upper Ridge area, stills are usually operated by a man and his male descendants. Women and children are in the know regarding family stills and often serve on sentry duty. However, inside knowledge on the part of persons outside the close family lines (even in-laws) constitutes a real threat.

The requirements for a still are these:

1. Private location on someone's farm—. The inaccessible, privately owned, densely-wooded coves are the best locations. A still needs a protected entrance yet needs to be fairly convenient to a widely traveled road where haulers will not attract attention.

2. Materials and equipment for making the whiskey—. Copper pipe is readily available from any plumber; odd pieces of dairy equipment and car junk, such as old radiators, are used for condensation. A good water supply is no problem in the hills; neither is firewood. The corn is raised, and the small amount of sugar needed is bought.

3. Maintenance of the still—. Usually the owners of the location, or the sons or brothers of the owners, manage the mash and fuel. One man can keep a still running; a man and his son are considered ideal for the job.

4. Protection of the still—. Stills are protected in two ways: first, by actual sentry duty, and second by a circulation of stories. Constant sentry duty is required at times, as when a still is smoking heavily. Everyone knows that intruders are not allowed to walk up certain paths. As one informant put it, "You walk around there and you get your hat shot off, or a bullet whistles by your ear." In addition to such knowledge, stories are told to control privacy of particular sections. Stories include phantom figures who live in specified hollows, haunted stumps, crying babies, creaking rockers, ghosts that

follow persons who walk after dark. For example, no one in the valleys can be persuaded to walk over a Ridge hill after sundown. When the writer's sons made such a walk, they were frightened, but unharmed, by a man who appeared out of the bushes carrying a gun. Often stills are established near isolated family graveyards. Some men manage their stills at night after a day's work. Although still workers supposedly take advantage of others' superstitions, they are usually superstitious themselves. And in a community where no one except bootleggers gets out on foot after dark, and the bootleggers halfway believe their own stories, the moonshining personnel itself may be in for some scares.

5. Outlet for the produce—. Most stills have pickup stations right where the whiskey is made, the stations being open only to a very few trusted buyers and haulers. Those who haul and sell bootleg whiskey keep the job through many generations. Certain family lines have always been heavily in the business of transporting and selling, but not making, the whiskey.

Men like to tell stories about the sly ways liquor is distributed. The following story was told after church one night:

There's the smartest ole man you ever seen that peddles bootleg in _____. Bunch of us was laughin' on the street corner th' other day 'bout the deputy tryin' to catch him. The ole man walked up, and one of us told the deputy, "Yonder comes yore whiskey man." So the deputy says to him, "Could you take this ten and find me some whiskey?" The ole man said, "I shore ken, and so you'll know I ain't run off with yore ten, you hole this pair o' shoes I bought till I get back here." We was wise, but the deputy stood there half the afternoon waitin'. Finally one of us says, "Why doncha take a look at them shoes yo're holdin'?" He unwrapped the shoebox, and there it was—two pints.

Bootleggers traditonally hand out free Sunday School literature wrapped around their wares, work through paper routes, grocery delivery, and so on.

Many stories are told of men who have "disappeared" in

Big Rook hills. When the minister mentioned that his station wagon had been stopped and searched on two nights during a revival, one local resident said:

I could walk to two stills from right here blindfolded. One's been thar forty years. No one's goin' up to it, either. While back, durin' a crackdown, a deputy come up to the house and says to a boy playin' out front, "Son, I'll give you $20 if you'll take me to the still; I need some whiskey." The boy, he kept playin'. The man says, "Will ye?" The boy says, "I'm wettin for you to give me the twenty, 'cause if you go thar, you ain't comin' back."

When the minister asked directions to some of his parishioners' homes in Big Rook, he was told by one who had lived at the entrance of a hollow for thirty years and never once traveled the road leading into it, "Anybody had better watch out how they turn into people's houses up there."

We can see from the foregoing work description how tobacco farming might be carried on with very little leadership; but where there are certain coveted business locations and where outlets are necessary for a product, as in bootlegging, some leadership positions are inevitable.

Leaders and External Relations

Forking off a new state highway in southeastern Kinbrace County is a gravel road which "dead ends" into some of the thickest still territory along the Tennessee Valley Divide. A county map of the area looks like this:

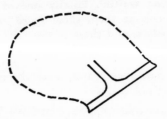

Sitting at this crossroad is the home of the man who in upper-Ridge territory enjoys by far the most notoriety and the highest prestige.

He is a member of one of the oldest and most beloved family lines in the hills. He was preceded in his leadership position by his father's brother, whose daughter he married. He and family members before him have long been in the social structure of the community and have played well the combined role of natural and representative leader for a large area.

Beside this influential leader, some institutional, daily-functional leaders exist throughout the territory. In upper-Ridge valleys one finds two unique leader types engaged in the still business. One is the man who is in a position of power because he owns important still locations and entrances such as an area of wooded land situated advantageously for operating, protecting, or distributing purposes. This leader's word carries weight among his neighbors, but he is usually hated personally and criticized publicly for "having too much land" or "getting too many possessions" or "thinking he is better than the rest of us."

In contrast, the other leader in a still community is loved and highly respected. He is both contact and distribution man for the community (and often for a large part of the county). He knows the locations of the nearby stills as well as the process by which their overflow finds its way to the county seat and larger towns. His home is always an important pickup point for information, sometimes for the liquor itself. In the still business, this second type of leader stands efficiently between the production and consumption units. His position has even greater social significance. Not only does he stand between the producer of the hills and county consumers; he also stands between open violators of the law and the county sheriff and deputies.

In particular, the second leader serves in the added capacities of appeaser and safety man for the community. He knows the law and those who violate it. He hobnobs with the sheriff's deputies and with the still men. He is respected by county officials, loved by locals. About him it is said: "He helps everyone"; "he would haul you all night if you needed him to"; "he's the best man I ever know'd"; "he's never let one of us down." At the same time, county officials depend on him. As one official explained, "He always knows where the legal violators are, and when they won't listen to anyone else they will listen to him tell them what they need to do to get right with the law." Such a leader regularly acts as bondsman for Ridge kinsfolk. In fact, the large number of services he performs reminds one of the work of "Honest John" in the Little Abner cartoon. As security man for illicit parts of the social structure, he hauls people or liquor; he can arrange to bury, to marry, to locate, or to dislocate; he bails out neighbor and kinsman. The obvious fact is that both county officials and upper-Ridge residents realize the necessity of such a position.

It is clear that leadership in Big Rook and Turnabout Hollow stems from two sources: distribution of the power and means for production, and distribution of the product and faculties for consumption. The leader in the unrespected role controls an excess amount of the means of production; the leader in the endeared role acts to integrate the illegal substructure with other community structure and with the larger political structure. As Erving Goffman describes discrepant roles, the revered representative leader comes nearest the role of go-between, whose function is to bring two obligatorily hostile elements to mutually profitable agreement.[1]

From these descriptions we can add that upper-Ridge families, with their moonshining, have goals and adaptations that involve more of the "outside world" than Applecross-Millstone families. Liquor for home consumption can be made in very isolated hollows, but moonshining as a business re-

1. *The Presentation of Self in Everyday Life*, p. 149.

quires roads and communication for transporting and selling the product.

Not only does the representative leader above the Ridge have more county-wide contact, but so do the other farming residents. The writer went to the county-seat square in the summer of 1962 to see whether there were many from the Ridge territory in attendance at Governor Clement's campaign speech. Only one man was present from Applecross-Millstone, and he was not listening to the speech but was sitting on the grass behind the courthouse. Nine adults were there from Turnabout Hollow, however, and seven from other Big Rook territory. Several Turnabout residents gathered around Clement after his speech and talked with him. One Turnabout woman said she wanted to meet him because she and he had a mutual friend. More Turnabout adults vote, take newspapers and magazines than do Applecross-Millstone adults. In fact, an Applecross informant said that she and two others were the only ones in her community who voted in the last election and that she alone took a daily paper. Thus the area below the Ridge better fits Parsons's description of the particularistic-ascriptive society in that external relations are more nearly ignored there.[2]

2. Talcott Parsons, *The Social System*, p. 198.

7. The Deme's Values

APPLECROSS-MILLSTONE also goes to an extreme in providing an example of another of Parsons's characteristics of a particularistic-ascriptive society.[1] It definitely prefers to keep status distinctions to a minimum. A man who was born and still resides five miles from Applecross, who married an Applecross girl and is active in the Methodist church there, observed:

> Slide Hill's different from any other place I ever saw; people there are all just the same. No one wants to get ahead of anyone else. No one is up high where others think he's high. It is sort of like the Northern Methodist communities that have the idea that everyone ought to be equal.

The observations of this man, who is near but slightly outside the Applecross structure, seem clear and accurate.

When the Applecross-Millstone adults were asked questions about community leadership, some surprising attitudes were revealed. On being probed concerning community problems and emergencies and those capable of handling them, men and women answered: "I don't know of no one 'round here like that." "I've never seen it tried here." "No need for such around here." "We jest all work together and holp our neighbors when they need us." One man said sneeringly that if he had gone to school a little longer maybe he could go around "takin' up collections and tellin' folks what to do, and the like."

1. Talcott Parsons, *The Social System*, p. 198.

At the time of the study, a man described as a community "pusher" was trying to persuade residents to let the county repair and widen the road through their valley. The man might have succeeded, but when the time came to stake off rights-of-way, he had obviously antagonized residents by bragging about what he was doing for the community. One resident approached the surveyors with her shotgun and told them that if they came back someone was liable to get killed. She pulled up the stakes and threw them over the fence after the men.

As the present study progressed, it became evident that negative feelings are attached to bragging, ambition, leadership, higher formal education, and that these status-related factors are all very closely connected in the minds of Applecross-Millstone members.

Residents were asked whether they thought a boy with a high school education would make a better husband and a better community member. Only three of the sixty-two adults said that perhaps he would do better at both; twelve said he would *not* make a better husband, but he might make a better community member, and forty-seven said he would do worse at both. Many of the answers said in effect, "More education makes for community leadership, and we're not in favor of either." The contents of the answers show strong valences.

The meanest people I know are the most educated. A man that's never had no schooling is afraid to get into meanness, but a educated man ain't afraid of no kind of meanness.

Some folks is too smart.

What most of us needs is some common sense. A man's got to come to his right knowin'.

Sometimes it's a disadvantage to have a education when yo're livin' in a community.

A boy with a high school education might do some things, but he don't know what bein' a husband's all about.

Nine out of ten doesn't know as much and makes better husbands. And a educated girl can't walk 'round a brier bush without gettin' scratched.

Education don't help one in bein' true and faithful. The kind of boy he is is what's important.

A educated man is contrary in his ways. Uneducated folks is more accommodatin'.

I've seen those that finished that done worse than others.

Jes' 'cause a boy's been to school don't mean he's legible [eligible].

You know what folks is learning at school these days? Well, ain't learning a thing but readin', writin', and rapscallion.

Why, a forty-year-old man come here the other day and was scared to death of my Jenny—says, "What's that? What makes its ears so long?"

Perhaps the two answers which most accurately express the desire to minimize status distinctions are:

A boy with education might get out and meet people and lead in the church and stuff, but he wouldn't be as good jest for an ordinary person.

A boy who finished high school might know more, but a plain old boy would come nearer being so-so.

A positive religious value is also related in community members' minds to low educational status. Preachers are "hurt more than helped," according to them, by going to seminary. One woman who had large sections of the Bible committed to memory said all she ever studied was a blue-back speller and the Scriptures and that all she knew was "a gift of God." Another man thought children these days

were getting "smarter and weaker." "They can read in the
first grade now, but the more they get in their minds, the
less they got in their hearts."

A seventy-year-old man reached in his overalls' pocket
and pulled out eye glasses which had one eye piece missing and
the other mended in two places. "I enrolled as a scholar in
the primer," he said. "You call it first grade now. Well, I
went through the primer." He hesitated. "I went through
the primer twice. When I went to courtin' I got tired of havin'
to ask my brothers to read my love notes, so I got busy and
learnt to read and write." The man's favorite joke is: "There
was eight of us boys and we each had a sister apiece." When
asked, "You mean there were eight girls too?" he laughs tri-
umphantly, "No, one girl."

Along with the dangers seen in education and leadership
come dangers related to getting ahead economically. It is a bad
sign for a man to be fast and efficient and ambitious. There
is a mule in the community that is highly criticized for being
"too fast." The writer's seventeen-year-old son, after working in the tobacco fields for several weeks, was likewise criticized for working too fast: "Why, he'd git everything he
could out of a day, then another inch." Upon hearing an
apology for possibly interrupting something important in the
middle of the day, one respondent drawled, "Done kilt the
day anyhow." Men pride themselves in being slow and sure,
in being satisfied with what they have, and in not working
after they consider themselves too old to work.

**He's too ole to work, but he works anyway. That man would
do anything fur a dollar.**

**That feller is never satisfied—always pushin'. If he had three
acres of tobacco to cut, he'd want it cut in one day.**

**I never owned a car or tractor. I farmed from the time I was
six years old, and I made fifty-six tobacco crops. I got all my
livin' out of fifty acres, dug it out of the dirt. I raised twelve**

kids, but every one of 'em got crossed up, tryin' to make money.

If sociologists identify the American success ideology as the desire to achieve wealth and status, we appropriately can apply the term "nonsuccess ideology" to the norms of our community.

Sociometric Choices

Certainly the absence of recognized leadership is another important expression of the value the deme places on keeping status distinctions to the minimum. This is plain from the sociometric part of the questionnaire, which asked for eight choices—the persons with whom the informant most and least preferred to work, the persons with whom he most and least preferred to spend free time, the persons whose advice he would most and least prefer to seek, and the persons he considered most and least capable of handling valley problems. More than half the informants refused to answer some or all of the sociometric questions, but out of the 230 total choices made in Applecross-Millstone, only one person was chosen as many as a total of eight times. Within the eight groups of answers (averaging thirty total answers per question), there were only three choices with as many as four persons agreeing on them, six choices on which three persons agreed, and eleven choices on which two persons agreed. Sociometric choices were within the valley but showed no significant patterning and no group preferences.

Thirty-eight respondents answered the question, "To whom would you go for advice?" and no one in the community except the minister was named more than once. The minister was named twice. The most interesting result from this part of the questionnaire is that the only men named several times (4, 3, and 3 choices out of 34 choices) as persons most capable of handling community problems are three men who have tried and failed to push through community improvements, men who are held in low esteem and live at the edge of the valley boundaries. They do not really "belong" to the deme.

In answer to the question, "Who do you think is *least* capable of handling community problems?" an older man apparently did not want to show favoritism. He replied, "So many of 'em that I don't know which to say." His response was recorded but not understood as complimentary until it was seen later in the nonleadership context.

It would be well to consider at this point the case of the person in Applecross-Millstone who received more favorable sociometric choices than any other (and as was stated above, this was only eight out of a possible 230). She is the widow residing in the old stone homestead. She was named for her grandmother Abiatha who died on the wagon trail returning from Texas; but she is referred to, almost reverently, as "Miss Abbie." The reader will recall that a woman's first name or nickname preceded by "Miss" is consistently reserved as a title indicating the very deepest respect joined with the closest intimacy.

The ascriptive rather than achievement criteria are clear in Miss Abbie's situation: she was born and has always lived in the valley; she is the oldest of several siblings living near her; she is closely or distantly related to almost all persons around her; she lives in the geographical center of the Applecross-Millstone area; there is no "foreign" element in her family lines nor in the lines of her marriage choice. According to the norms of the community, she married young, married her senior, and married a second cousin, once removed. She is reserved, neat, individually expressive, and she possesses "the inner strength" that valley families say is needed for the "burdens of this life." Like other valley residents, she gives the impression of knowing who she is and of avoiding all appearances of artificiality.

A puzzling thing is that Miss Abbie is the only valley person mentioned in the parent image. Time and again, residents have said, "Miss Abbie is a second mother to me." One woman, twenty years older than Miss Abbie, made the statement and then told how Miss Abbie gave her and others food when articles were rationed during the Second World War. A younger woman who saw her in this light had lived with Miss Abbie during the war. Two couples who have operated Applecross Store, owned by Miss Abbie, spoke of her giving without expecting in return. This particular community bond stands uniquely as a nonreciprocal, strong, vertical-type bond in an otherwise horizontally knit community. Miss Abbie, it seems, is a mother ideal for the Applecross-Millstone families. Like others in the community, she takes part in all interaction processes, careful not to assume leadership. The bond between her and her neighbors is one of esteem rather than prestige, of love joined with nonreciprocal instrumental relations. It is a bond of respect, lacking in attempts at segregation.

Church Organization and Music

The feeling against authorized leadership and the strong, expressive, individualistic tendencies in Ridge territory are evident at religious meetings. "Sins" and disappointments are specifically named at the church altar. Excessive crying is frowned upon but happens at every worship service. One girl who committed sex offenses dreaded going back to her parents. "They will want me to go to church and then everyone will cry over me." Individual repentance, the bearing of one another's burdens, and a divine power giving legitimization to all activity are continuing and strong themes among the church laymen. A ninety-year-old woman expressed her faith in a divine power: "If God is fur you, nothin' is aginst you. They ken cut off your haid and turn you 'round, and if God's fur you, he'll put it back on."

There is sincere interest in church school and worship, but there is very little institutionalized leadership. Persons hesitate to accept traditional church offices. They prefer "just to all do it together." They resent "higher" church representatives such as the Methodist district superintendent. They resent "orders that are handed down to the small church." And, in turn, persons in connectional authority lament the fact that "there is no leadership in these rural churches." On that criterion, doors to a very live egalitarian church are sometimes closed. As indicated in the dedication of this book, one might say that such an organization does not dwindle and die but is killed in the conflict and confusion of norms.

From the administration standpoint, valley churches, like other rural ones, expect a warm, communal type of pastoring; they want most for their preachers to eat with them, be one of them, join them for dinner on the grounds, sing and talk long hours with them. This is in contrast to the formal kind of ministry expected from urban congregations —visitation on certain occasions and celebrations, participation in community clubs and campaigns, efficient administration and leadership training related to church offices.

The best loved pastors, and those under whose ministry valley churches thrive, are the part-time supply men. These men are often farmers who receive their "call to preach" later in life and their ordination after completing a shortcut correspondence study instead of attending seminary. A seminary education and a highly paid ministry strongly go against the rural ideal of a preacher who is trained by the Holy Spirit and stores up treasures in Heaven. Dynamic leadership techniques are not in keeping with the ideal pastoral role of suffering servant. Also out of keeping with this role are a minister's efforts to promote the latest institutional programs with up-to-date equipment. Some ministers who have unwittingly divorced themselves from rural congregations by meeting professional standards attempt to rectify the damage by engaging in part-time farming, driving older model cars, or wearing older style clothes. The minister and his family must, however, be sincere in appreciation and preference for the so-so ways, since valley residents are quick to recognize discrepancies and conspicuous nonconsumption.[2]

It is often hard to tell who is the adult teacher in a valley church school. The adult classes always read their church school lesson, a paragraph per person, then read and answer each question at the end of the lesson. Conceivably this is a conscious or unconscious leveling technique of a group that is making an effort to keep leadership in the background. It may be that part of the negative feeling toward education is a resentment against the authoritative situation in a classroom.

Church singings are a vital part of the religious life of Ridge families. Singing participants pride themselves on being interdenominational "except for Church of Christ and Roman Catholic." Gospel songs are sung from cheap paperback books, using shaped-note songbooks from Stamps Quartet or James Vaughn music publishers. Large numbers of the books are bought with money from collections taken at the singings and then carried home to become part of the family collection of "good old songs." These gospel songs usually have variations of the themes of free salvation and help for all men, the great need for love and prayer, heavenly joys and riches versus present sorrow and deprivation. Most of the words have a personal emphasis rather than the theological emphasis of denominational hymnals found in urban churches. The hymns are rousing and emotional, reflecting the same leveling appeals found in Negro spirituals. One woman expressed gratitude that a crippling injury had occurred at

2. It is no wonder that rural congregations, as well as a few clergymen, have grave reservations about current movements to render the ministry even more professional and to reorganize and combine parishes in order that every pastor be a seminary man, fill a full-time ministerial position, and draw an annual salary of $7,000 or more.

From the divide

Goats in a typical valley setting

Hillside pastures

Across the valley

The tobacco seedbed

Taking a break

Top: Old ways hang on

Bottom: The modern touch

It used to be a schoolroom

The old school

Public road

A valley farm

The oldest church

Women's privy

Men's privy

Churchyard bench

church rather than somewhere else. She began singing, "I must tell Jesus all of my troubles. I cannot bear my burdens alone," after which she began to shout, adding, "When I sing that song, I have to holler."

Solos are rare in this type of music. A solo, in fact, is considered "show off." If one is requested by a member of the audience the singer characteristically asks several others to come forward to help. Interplaying soprano, alto, tenor, and bass solo parts are frequent within a quartet, but these parts fit into rather than stand out from the whole. The ideal singings have large sections of all four parts and, most important of all, "real heart-felt singing by everyone."

Shaped-note singing is so designed that any child or adult may learn the fundamentals in a two-weeks singing school. Shortcut methods of "chord-melody" piano instruction make it possible for a pianist of only a few months to accompany. Well-trained voices are not held in high esteem for singing convention music. The emphasis is placed on willingness to sing. At some time during every singing someone is likely to remind the group that "we are singing with the spirit as well as with the understanding." This same ideal applies to the playing of the piano and of other musical instruments. Actually, the rhythm is more important in playing and singing valley hymns than the words and the correct notes.

Individuality and creativity in manner of playing and singing, such as harsh and grating tone quality, blaring loudness, facial contortions, piping falsettos, crying while singing, musical lilts to the last words of phrases, are highly desirable. One has the feeling there is a conscious effort to be unlike trained musicians. In this community activity, at least, singers seem to enjoy abandonment, entirely free of inhibitions or emotional restraints.

Pianist, leaders, and quartets constantly rotate during a singing. The announcer for the convention or the leader of the singing school makes sure that everyone who will lead a song or take part in a special number does so. The best singing school leader is the one who gets everyone of every age to take his turn in directing the singing. Leaders, pianists, and quartets are presented in rather strict order. If after one complete round is made a leader or quartet gets up front again, this calls for another complete round.

Sins and Disappointments

The institution of the local church, embodying as it does the deme, operates more effectively below the Ridge in tension-releasing, legitimizing, leveling, and convicting processes than it does above. This is to be expected, considering the differences in church attendance, in tightness of structure, and in community cohesion. Yet the verbalized values are very much the same in the two areas. What are the "sins" and disappointments that valley residents carry to their church altar?

The greatest disappointments to valley people are ill health and death. Material losses are never mentioned as disappointments. A plausible explanation of this, as well as the fact that love losses are seldom mentioned, is that persons suffering such losses either take violent action and then leave the valley (by suicide, homicide, or migration), or they accept the situation and conform to the deme's norm of being contented with their lot. Older residents often say, "I'm gettin' awfully old and weak. This old house is gonna last longer than I am."

To let anything less than sickness and death divide families is considered a sin. For family members to go out of the community to make money is a sin, not a disappointment. Fighting with neighbors and illicit sex are the greatest local sins, for they have the most disruptive power. The greatest world sin is war between nations because "it cuts into families, takes away the young men—it's an awful sin." [3]

3. Ridge men, however, are noted for making good soldiers. For example, the Purple Heart was awarded in 1945 to one Ridge paratrooper who jumped from a C-45 over the Rhine and was put out of action by a

Choosing from a set of six conditions generally considered "wrong," (see question 34 of the questionnaire), respondents listed them in order from "most wrong" to "least wrong." Seventy-six percent considered a sexually promiscuous woman as most wrong, but no one considered a sexually promiscuous man as most wrong. Twelve percent thought it most wrong to fight with one's neighbors, and the *degree* of wrongness for a man who fights with his neighbors was 22 percent higher than for a man who is unfaithful to his wife. Six percent viewed a woman who said untrue things in court as most wrong.

A double-standard sex norm is evident throughout the Ridge. For example, Ego and her husband blamed X, their son's wife, but not Y, their daughter's husband, who were "caught laying in," the expression used for an illicit sex act. As shown in the chart below, Y is more kin than X is to Ego.

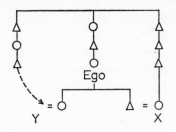

FIG. 15—*An illicit act.*

In sex talk, it is the woman who is pictured as the assailant. On a cold night, a resident was manning a Christmas tree stand when a female acquaintance approached him. "You need heat," he quoted her as saying. "Woman," he replied, "I got heat—two big cans of coal, two full pints of whiskey. I don't need yore heat."

machine gun bullet, hid out in German trenches, crawled up steep banks, killed three German soldiers, and finally made his way to a United States Army hospital in England.

Any wife who does not keep up with her homemaking tasks is a sex suspect, as represented by such remarks as, "She lies around on a couch like a queen." "You orta see all the knickknacks that woman buys." ("Knickknacks" are ready-prepared food, such as lightbread.) "Why, she wouldn't even iron her husband a shirt to go see a corpse." (If a man ever needs a ironed shirt, it's "t'see a corpse.") On the other hand, no one ever condemns a husband who evades his work. If anything, a man who sits around home a lot blesses a family group. A "roving husband" or a "rambling man" is a real disappointment. Respectable people stay indoors after dark. Roving at night is a sin. When families visit one another or go to the store they make sure they get there "by the edge of dark." Church and other get-togethers are set for "the edge of dark."

Roving, whoring, brawling, cutting, killing, gambling with dice, heavy drinking (but not moonshining), are "wrong" and are considered "Big Rook." It's "Big Rook" to be suspicious of neighbors or to carry firearms constantly. To shoot too freely is "Big Rook." Speeding is "Big Rook." To tell sex jokes to women, to talk loudly and profanely before women is "Big Rook," though rough talk is always acceptable among men and boys and is facilitated by sex segregation at all gatherings.

One of the most respectable activities for men is to loaf and loiter with other men. The only acceptable game is horseshoes, but it is just played by young men. Baseball is somewhat allowable for young men, but Sunday baseball is a sin. According to the study's prediction for a nonachievement, noncompetitive society, Ridge families frown on the playing of games. Asked whether they would rather play games with neighbors or sing or visit, they answered, "I never was raised up to gaming—no kind of rook or cards." "A few of the men play a little pedro in the winter here, but I go home when they start." "I don't believe in no games; only ones I ever played was at a shower once. My husband isn't religious, and even he won't play games. He don't believe in shorts or women wearing men's clothes either."

As to women's dress, they do not wear pants or slacks, but they often cut up men's dungaree pants to make themselves work skirts. The most evident difference in female attire is the hair, which is cut very short and curled very tightly. Women give each other home permanents or go to a beauty parlor several miles away. A favorite style is hair that is fresh washed, unrolled, and in short ringlets. It was some time before the writer realized that consciously or unconsciously "loose hair" means a "loose woman." Two Ridge ladies were overheard to say about an outsider, "She can't be much; look at that long, stringy hair." One wonders why the women in the community with the loosest sex morals do not cut and curl their hair to avoid suspicion. It may be they are more intent on pleasing the men, or they may be, again consciously or unconsciously, conforming to the role expectations others have of them.

Bragging is a sin. One husband said that the worst part of his wife's behavior was that she bragged about her sexual conquests to neighbors. The reader will recall that plans for the new road right-of-way failed because a resident bragged about what he was doing for the community. One typical Ridge song leader never says, "We'll sing number —," but always, "I'm all choked down and all stove up today, and I'm no song leader anyhow, but we're gonna try to sing number—." The only safe thing to talk about is others, unless the talk about oneself is extremely modest, even belittling. To say, "Did you know Frank's down in his back again?" means the speaker is concerned about Frank.

An unconcerned, a cold-hearted, or a strict and autocratic person is a sinner. In fact, a "cold-hearted sinner" is a man who is so strict on his wife and children that he will not let them come to church, or a man who is "stingy and mean" to his own family. It is not a man's disbelief in scriptural doctrine but the way he acts toward his family that marks him as a "cold-hearted sinner." Likewise, a "cold-blooded murderer" is a man who shoots a close kinsman, as his son or his brother. Recently one of the laymen above the Ridge was persuaded to speak to a lower-Ridge church. His topic was "The Darkest Hour in History," which he defined as the day Cain killed his brother Abel. Not being warm toward one's own is thus a sin—"cold-blooded" if it kills, "cold-hearted" if it affects the living.

The main distinction which valley residents make between the religious and the nonreligious is whether a person believes in the power of prayer to soften one's heart and to bring about miracles of love. Church members testify that prayer is the one channel open to them in the delicate interactions between close kin. Prayer warms the hearts of those who offer it toward those for whom they pray. The plea, "Pray for me," means, "Don't hold anything against me." Or, "Pray for those we love," means "Be on guard as to your feelings toward these persons." Accordingly, prayer may be an exceedingly powerful tool for the deme's internal peace and good will.

The greatest sin of omission is to fail to be helpful to members of the deme. The one man below the Ridge who confided that he would like to move said it was because "my neighbor looks out for hisself too much, doesn't appreciate old-fashioned ways of helping, and tries to be a big man in the church." Here are named the sins of ambition, egotism, and failure to help neighbors.

Neighbor relations, as will be seen in the following section, are of utmost importance and sometimes touchy. In an informal conversation, an Applecross man said, "Lyin's bad, stealin's worse, but there's nothin' worse than for a man to have trouble with neighbors." When the most easily offended man in Applecross was asked to classify the list of "wrongs" in the questionnaire, he shouted: "I get along *fine* with my neighbors; I'm not gonna say *anything* against *anybody*."

Friends, Neighbors, and Kin

It is hard to determine how often deme members see one another. An interviewee first said that the last time she and her brother, a neighbor, got together was seven months ago, at Christmas; then she added that he checked in every week or so but they were all "so busy." Later she mentioned that he brought hay that morning and ate lunch with her family and stayed a couple of hours. A seven-year-old daughter corrected her mother when the mother said she never talked with her cousin, a neighbor, exclaiming that they just finished a conversation which took "half the morning."

In the same way that these occasions are not considered "visits," valley persons are never called "friends." A fellow member of the deme is a neighbor or a relative. The word "friend," which is seldom heard, refers to persons who live elsewhere. Around the dinner table, one of the writer's sons said people should be fair to their friends, and the Apple-cross host looked puzzled, then replied, "Yes, folks should do right by friends—if you can find out who your friends are." A woman who works part-time in Fraserburgh lunch-room said she had a "friend" there who "just fell in love with me—no kin." Two "friends" that were mentioned during the study live in Nashville and in California; about both it was said, "We used to be neighbors, raised up and worked together." A "friend" is one who does not have the status of neighbor or kin, is outside the deme, but is still in warm contact with the speaker.[4] Applecross-Millstone residents rarely use the word, for their "friends" are few; Turnabout Hollow residents more often speak of friends in the county seat, Nashville, or nearby towns.

4. My husband regarded the following statement as the highest compliment he received from a valley parishioner: "Me and my wife was talkin' last night. And I says, 'Mae, that preacher's not like a friend to me. He's like one of my own family, like my brother. It's as though I'd know'd him always—and him a rank stranger.'"

The valley emphasis on "neighbor" rather than "friend" fits well in a rural system attempting to minimize status differences. In a stratified system, one expects friends to be highly selected, largely from occupational strata. In a deme, one's associates are one's kin and neighbors, and these have the added characteristic of being given. Here the analogy between friend and neighbor is the same as between achievement and ascription. Unpublished tables of the Southern Appalachian study show that urban churches are more composed of friends and rural churches of kin.

It is important for neighbors to get along in the valley. The urgency is felt and expressed this way: "Can't have no racket with neighbors. I've been livin' in this valley all my life, and I never knowd no scrappin' or disorder amongst those gathered." "You gotta learn to love yore neighbors— anyone you work with. If you can't get along, get out."

The question was asked whether persons should expect more of their "close kin" than of "just friends and neighbors." Forty percent of the respondents replied in the affirmative, but each of these responses was seasoned with such statements as, "but I have awful good neighbors," "but you ought to be nice to all your neighbors," "but neighbors mean lots," "but neighbors are hard to beat." The other 60 percent said persons should be able to expect just as much from neighbors: "Neighbors are closer." "If I need something, I'd ask someone who's close rather than go way off." "No, everyone ought to love everybody." "No, I stick if I am or ain't kin." Judging from the strict norm of reciprocity, the most honest reply was probably, "I would do as much fur a neighbor that was good to me as I would fur kin." Many, of course, pointed out that their neighbors are their kin.

A question designed to get information on the community's attitude toward outside authority and to measure the extent to which persons employ universal standards of judgment furnished valuable information regarding kin and neighbor. Three-fourths of the Applecross-Millstone residents said they would go to the law if there were young people from Nashville stealing gasoline from them. "That's the onliest way." Some said, "Law wouldn't do nothing." But not one of the sixty-two residents said he would go to the law if the violators were children of neighbors and close kin.

If children of their neighbors, most residents would go to the children themselves first, then the parents. There were such replies as, "I'd talk to the children before I told the parents; I don't believe in causin' no one trouble." "If they were my neighbor's children, I'd just hold together with them; I'd not be the one to tell it." "I believe in doin' to others as you'd have them do to you." "I'd go to the parents, but I'd take a lot first; if you did turn them over to the law, the law would only get them into more trouble, and your neighbors would turn against you." One woman even said, "I'd apologize to them, I reckon."

Toward children of close kin some residents would do the same as toward neighbors' children, but the following distinctive answers were given: "I'd spank them." "I'd take a limb to them." "It would break my heart." "I'd just go to the Lord." "I'd try to show them what's right." Evidently, in considering neighbors' children the person is concerned about his relation with the parents; whereas in considering children of close kin he is thinking of the correction and training of the offenders. The "Golden Rule" is more often expressed and reciprocity is more of a requirement where neighbors are concerned. It will be recalled that there was giving without return connected with the mother image (which is the primary kin relation) in the "Miss Abbie" ideal.

A statement (see question 39 of the questionnaire) designed to test whether persons have a desire to learn new things was answered with more references to neighbors. To the statement, "Some folks say 'I'm not interested in hearing a lot of arguments with which I do not really agree,' " the uni-

versal response was, "I don't believe in arguin' with my neighbors either." Half way through the questionnaire the word
"arguments" was changed to "talk." This did not change the
answer. "Talk" in the valley apparently means "malicious
talk" or "untruth," for the answers continued: "I'm not interested in stuff like that." "A lot of talk goes on I'm not fur
a bit." "I don't like gossip." "I have my way of doin'; when
politicians and courts start holdin', I'd rather be somewhere
else." "Talk between neighbors may start as a joke, then
spread to killings."

The majority of persons named their neighbors when they
were asked for the three persons or families they would invite
for a get-together at their home. Many just replied, "All my
neighbors; I wouldn't leave out a one of my neighbors." One
man complained that his neighbor A (who is married to his
second cousin) had no fences and let the buck weeds take
everything. He added, "If 'twas mine, I'd take a brush ax
to cleanin' them out. An' I keep good fences, 'cause a good
fence makes a good neighbor." However, he named A first
as one he would invite to a social at his home. At many
of the homes the illustration had been used, "Suppose you
were having an ice cream supper or the like, what three persons or families would you invite?" Though the ice cream
illustration was not given in this particular interview, the
interviewee volunteered, "A doesn't like ice cream, but I'd
ask him anyway." At the following visit, information as to
the number of names desired was purposely withheld, but the
respondent said confidently, "You want three names, doncha?" Such answers point to problems in validity but also
reveal the connected communication networks of neighbors
in a closed community.

Some of the most constant jokers of the community are
neighbors who have obvious personality clashes and who maintain safe distances in this manner. Several such pairs start
calling loudly to each other as soon as they get within hearing

distance. In order to maintain the cohesion essential to a corporate deme, it is important that neighbors get along. As we shall see in the following chapter, however, there are structural deficiencies in some areas that lead to violence instead of peace.

8. Structural Strain

L ET us take a brief look at the historical and geographical facts connected with violence around Duck River Ridge. Formerly there was a road on top of the Ridge. The old road has recently interested Kinbrace County historians. All nearby roads intersected or were identified by it. Kinbrace County court minute records for the early 1800's are full of such references as the following:

Ordered that . . . mark and lay out a road the nearest and best way . . . to intersect the road cut by Federal troops at or North of the Duck River Ridge.

We have proceeded to view mark and lay off a road . . . crossing Murfree's fork . . . to a gap of Duck River Ridge.

Ordered that . . . oversee the cleaning out and keeping in repair the public road leading from . . . to . . . on Duck River Ridge.[1]

The Ridge has been an important natural dividing line. It separates census districts. It was an effective boundary between the Choctaw-Chickasaw tribes to the south and whites to the north. For about two or three hundred years previously, or until the early part of the eighteenth century, it served as the boundary between the Muskogian tribes (to which the Chickasaws and Choctaws belong and which comprised the region from the Gulf of Mexico to Middle Tennessee) and the Algonkian Shawnees, who split up when they were driven from Pennsylvania by the Iroquois, one group living for some

1. County *Court Minute Book* (1800–1812), pp. 48, 69, 98.

two hundred years above the Ridge along the Cumberland River in Tennessee and Kentucky, and a second group in the Carolinas.

Thus it appears that the Ridge has long been an important boundary. South of it the Muskogian tribes made peaceful pacts with the whites and became one of the constituents of the Five Civilized Tribes; north of it the Shawnees crusaded to unite all Indians against the whites. In an attempt to enlist five thousand Muskogees before the bloody 1811 attack, the Shawnee leader Tecumseh shouted, "Let the white man perish. . . . Burn their dwelllings! . . . Slay their wives and children! . . . War now! War forever!" [2]

In 1886 a history of Tennessee referred to Fraserburgh (two miles below the Ridge and two miles west of Applecross) as being a pleasant place to live, maintaining an academy, cultural interests, and community clubs. The same account gave the origin of the name "Grabbucks" or "Grabs," an early nickname for Buckeyville, two miles above the Ridge and north of Fraserburgh. The name originated in the fact that an individual grabbed ten dollars from his unsuspecting companion.[3]

Today, though integrated on lower levels than either the Choctaws and Shawnees or Fraserburgh and Buckeyville, Applecross and Millstone below the Ridge have good reputations, whereas Turnabout Hollow and Big Rook above the Ridge have records of and reputations for violence. Close to Turnabout Hollow spatially and functionally, Big Rook is the most notorious trouble section near Duck River Ridge. If you ask residents of southeastern Kinbrace County where Big Rook is located, it is "just over the next hill," but the stills and violence which characterize it seem to cover most of the upper-Ridge section of the Tennessee Valley Divide.

2. Brewton Berry, *Race and Ethnic Relations*, p. 495; and Clark Wissler, *Indians of the United States*, pp. 79–83.

3. *History of Tennessee* (Nashville: The Goodspeed Publishing Co., 1886).

These historical data are not offered as an explanation of present-day violence but to show that certain upper-Ridge patterns have persisted for two hundred years. The activities, both of white upper-Ridge frontier settlers and of the upper-Ridge Shawnee tribe, suggest long-standing violent adaptation patterns in contrast to the nonviolent ones of early Indians and whites who settled below Duck River Ridge. No rational explanation of this continuity, however, can be given in terms of the Ridge's being a physical cause of social conditions. Nor can it rest on cultural continuity, since Indian and settler social systems presumably were entirely distinct and replaced each other in the territory.

Violence in the News

That an excessive amount of violence in upper-Ridge territory exists is based, not just on common knowledge through and around the Ridge itself, but on a survey of Kinbrace County newspapers from 1814 to the present time. The majority of Kinbrace County legal offenders reported in the news have familiar names, being living or deceased relatives of present residents in the upper-Ridge section studied, though this area is actually less than a sixth of the total area of Kinbrace County.

The two tables below summarize the newspaper survey. The last three columns of Table 3 show the stability, over ten-year periods, in the number of violence, murder, and suicide cases reported in the county paper and involving the deme names. Table 4 gives a basis for comparing the kind and amount of upper and lower Ridge violations occurring from 1930 to 1960.

Figures in the first two columns of Table 4 are for areas which are two miles wide (one area being two miles above and the other two miles below the Ridge line) and twelve miles long, extending to the county line at the east, two-thirds of the way to the county line at the west, and to the county line at the south. The territory reported in the third column

TABLE 3

Newspaper Cases Bearing Familiar Deme Names

Year	Convicted of Operating Stills or of Drunkenness	Accidents (Approximately Two-Thirds Fatal)				Violence (Not Followed by Death)	Murder	Suicide
		Gun	Fire	Car	Others			
Before 1922		2			2	3	2	1
1923–1932	15	1		1	3	10	9	5
1933–1942	6	4	2		1	9	10	10
1943–1952	3	1	1			4	9	4
1953–1962	2		3	8	2	7	10	6
Total	26	8	6	9	8	33	40	26

Note: Newspaper files before 1922 are incomplete. Where there are 32 microfilm reels of county newspapers since 1922, there is only one mixed reel of previous county papers. Some of the early issues are blurred and difficult to read; also, reporting for the area was scant before 1922.

TABLE 4

Newspaper Accounts of Certain Events, 1930–1960

	From Ridge to Two Miles Above Ridge for 12-Mile Stretch	From Ridge to Two Miles Below Ridge for 12-Mile Stretch	From Two Miles Above to Four Miles Above Ridge for 12-Mile Stretch
Murders	19	0	9
Suicides	10	6	4
Murder and Suicide	4	0	0
Operating Stills	12	1	8
Hit and Run Deaths	3	0	0
Jailbreaking	3	0	0
Check Forgery	3	0	3
TOTAL	54	7	24
Number of Households, 1960	230	202	230
Ratio of Offenses to Households [a]	1 in 4	1 in 30	1 in 10

lies, again, two miles north of the upper-Ridge stretch and extends twelve miles in length. For the sake of comparison, territory and population density are roughly the same for all three areas. Both areas above the Ridge contain 230 homes, and the area below contains 202 homes. Judging from the 1937 Kinbrace County geology map this density has not changed appreciably in the past thirty years.

The county newspaper figures do not represent the total number of these particular activities, but the written accounts

a. There would be slightly less difference between the ratios of offenses to residents because of different family fertility patterns.

are enough to support common local knowledge that upper-Ridge violence exceeds that of most areas. Since we have confidence in the population stability of this area and also in the stability of the number of homicide cases each decade, it is meaningful to compare the annual homicide rate for the 230 homes (or 1,150 persons) in the twelve-mile area just above the Ridge with national figures. The annual homicide rate for the designated upper-Ridge section is .633 per 1,150 persons, or 55 per 100,000 persons. This is, according to *Uniform Crime Reports for the United States,* five times higher than the annual rate for the east south central states during the same period, and eleven times higher than that for the United States in general.[4] Just as important for our purpose is the fact that, according to the newspaper breakdown of county violence, no homicide occurred in the twelve-mile stretch below the Ridge during the thirty years involved.

Is there any consistency in the relation of Ridge homicide victims to those who kill them? Does joking—another much-used form of tension release which may range from mild jesting to serious, persistent annoying—occur more often between certain positions? Both joking and violence against persons seem to take place most often between those whose ties through marriage predominate over their blood ties. Out of thirty pairs of persons who engage in the most evident joking relations, twenty are in-laws. The largest category of identifiable relations within the twenty-eight Ridge murders shown in Table 4 for 1930–1960 is the in-law category. In this category of nine killings are two father-in-law victims, two mother-in-law victims, a son-in-law and a brother-in-law victim. The table that follows is labeled according to the community or kin relation that appears primary. It shows that the illegality of moonshining is not sufficient to explain endemic violence in this area.

4. U.S. Department of Justice, Federal Bureau of Investigation, *Uniform Crime Reports for the United States,* XXVII, No. 2 (1956).

TABLE 5

Relation of Jokers and Slayer-Slain Pairs

Relation of 30 Most Evident Pairs of Jokers		Relation of 28 Pairs of Slayer And Slain (From Murder Category of Table 4)	
in-laws	20	in-laws	9
uncle-nephew	3	unidentified	6
cousins	2	former neighbors	3
neighbors	2	neighbors	2
aunt-nephew	1	gamblers	2
father-son	1	moonshiner-sheriff	1
brothers	1	father-son	1
		nephew-uncle	1
		uncle-nephew	1
		brothers	1
		husband-wife	1

Tense Relations

Uncles and aunts appear four times among the joking pairs in Table 5, and two of the murders involve uncles and nephews. In the section on forms of address, the peculiar valley use of "aunt" and "uncle" was pointed out. Specific information on the quality of the avuncular relation was secured from the questionnaire. Respondents were given a card with four lines on it (see question 49 of the questionnaire), each line numbered from 1 through 5 and representing the typical kind of relation between the following four sets of valley kin: husband-wife, father-son, brother-sister, and nephew-uncle. After it was explained that the number "1" meant completely free and informal, and the number "5" meant completely reserved and formal, respondents were asked to circle one of the five numbers for each set of relations. Applecross-Millstone adults responded with a total of six "5's," that is, with six "completely reserved" marks; and four of these were for nephew-uncle relations.

Mean markings were then computed for each of the kinship relations in order to test a kinship law that applies primarily to societies which count descent through only one parent. According to Lévi-Strauss the relation between maternal uncle and nephew is to the relation between brother and sister as the relation between father and son is to the relation between husband and wife.[5] That is, if one set of relations is different, the other is different; if one set is congruent, the other is congruent. This structural law, which as far as the writer knows has not been tested, is represented diagrammatically in this manner:

$$\triangle \overset{+}{\underset{+}{=}} \overset{-}{\bigcirc} \triangle \quad \triangle \overset{-}{\underset{-}{=}} \overset{+}{\bigcirc} \triangle \quad \triangle \overset{+}{\underset{-}{=}} \overset{+}{\bigcirc} \triangle \quad \triangle \overset{-}{\underset{+}{=}} \overset{-}{\bigcirc} \triangle$$

Note: The plus means a free and familiar relation, the minus means a relation of hostility, antagonism, or reserve.

Our statistical means for the four sets of relations are husband-wife, 1.6; father-son, 2.1; brother-sister, 1.8; nephew-uncle, 2.9. Thus 2.9:1.8=2.1:1.6. Even though the Lévi-Strauss law is for unilateral societies, it does not break down in our case.

The statistical means indicate that a person feels closer to his spouse or siblings than to his parents or children. According to this, as well as interaction data, collateral ties are warmer than lineal or vertical ties. It is not surprising, considering the reserved avuncular relations, that 90 percent of the Applecross-Millstone parents said they would trust their teenage daughter to go on an overnight trip with her uncle but not with an older cousin. One man winked and said he had been around long enough to know what went on between cousins. Another said he wouldn't even want his daughter with her older brother on an overnight trip.

As Table 5 reveals, in-law relations are the most explosive of any relations in the valley, as elsewhere. It may be that

5. Claude Lévi-Strauss, *Anthropologie Structurale*, pp. 51–55.

the emotional distance between uncle and nephew is in part due to the traditionally potential father and son-in-law relation between the two. Also, interaction between couples and their siblings' children declines as the children reach the age to marry. One Millstone woman explained that she didn't see her nieces and nephews much since they were grown or had families of their own, even though they lived as close to her as ever. This is not the case if there is a simulated parental tie between nieces or nephews and aunts or uncles; but when such a tie exists, the quality is emphasized by such a remark as, "She is more like my own daughter than my niece." One informant tried to make plain his attachment to an uncle by saying repeatedly during one interview, "He's much more like a brother to me than an uncle." But another informant proudly named over "all the kin" who lived near him, then added reluctantly, "Oh, there's my sister's boy too. He lives up the way."

Jokes and pranks are common forms of tension release between uncles and nephews. One man's nephew, back from the air force, told neighbors at the country store that he planned to put on his red flying suit and scare his uncle late some night. The uncle heard of his intentions and spread word among the same men that there had better be someone behind the nephew to pick him up when he fell. Another nephew rolled a flaming tire down a Ridge hill on his uncle; the uncle retaliated by shooting at the car as it rounded the curve. Still another nephew planted a stick of dynamite in a bush by his uncle's house. Several young nephews of one resident who had the habit of removing his hat as he went under a certain tree with low branches climbed the tree and showered their uncle's head with roasting corn as he passed. The deme is very lenient toward such "jokes" played by young people, even to hurling large rocks or setting off explosives from Ridge hills.

Apparently the greatest antagonisms result from a buildup of a number of tense relations. One man feels especially antagonistic toward two other men in his neighborhood—A and B. The man's grandfather married an A after his first wife died; the man's mother's brother and sister both married an A, and his father's brother married a third A sibling. As for the Bs, one of the man's father's sisters and two of his own girl cousins married them. A number of avuncular and in-law ties are thus involved in the antagonism toward these two men. On the other hand, a system which aids community relations is one in which persons who are related in multiple ways emphasize the kin tie viewed as most favorable. For example, one man calls his father's sister by an informal nickname rather than "aunt" and speaks of her as his cousin; she is actually his first cousin once removed through his mother.

Signs of Strain

Tense vertical relations such as the uncle-nephew ones, plus the feeling of urgency that is continually expressed for getting along with neighbors, may be construed as signs of strain in the deme's structure. Two other conditions should be viewed in this light also. They are the practices of runaway marriage and auctions, both examples of a family affair which has become a community event. In the one, parents have lost their power to assign sons or daughters in marriage; in the other, they have lost power to redistribute property through interfamily agreement.

Still another condition of the area should be discussed—a condition which, according to ethnographers, adds to the stress in a social system but at the same time aids in social control by releasing more tension than it creates.[6] This is the belief in witches and ghosts, and in certain persons and groups possessing supernatural power.

We have seen how the circulation of stories about ghosts,

6. Paul Bohannan, *Social Anthropology;* p. 349. Edward Norbeck, *Religion in Primitive Society,* pp. 192–193; and B. B. Whiting, *Paiute Sorcery,* pp. 80–81.

spirits after dark, or haunted territory helps maintain privacy
for moonshine operations. Even though still owners make
use of these beliefs, they and all the community are caught
up in many of the same fears. The writer attempted to compliment a resident's grown son with "I think he hung the
moon." "Oh, no," she replied quickly, "maybe the sun, but
not the moon; he never wuz out at that hour." The two-
hundred-pound son strengthened her statement with, "Owls
never strike at me. I stay in after dark." People often speak
of the owls and witches in Big Rook and of the women who
"can curse a man fur you."

One of the most powerful of these is a Negro woman who
lives just outside Turnabout Hollow. Her occult gifts, aided
by her use of cards and the Bible, are sought to predict the
manner of death or to help find lost objects. When a boy ran
away after a quarrel with his father, she was consulted. She
said he would return along a particular railroad but not to
look for him. Half accepting and half rejecting her advice,
the whole community gathered at the railroad siding to look
for the boy, who later returned of his own accord.

We have called the auctioneer a sort of scapegoat in that
where the family has forfeited to the deme the power to redistribute property the auctioneer bears the "sins" of the
transaction. In the same sense other persons and groups
in the valleys act as scapegoats by being linked to the stigmas
of disappointments and misfortunes or the stigma of deviation
from valley norms.[7] The Negro church in Turnabout Hollow,
made up of Negroes who live east in two small towns along
the new highway, has been referred to as an unwanted and
weird group. It bears the stigma of being socially different
and dangerous, but it has also a mysterious power: here is a

7. Some ethnographers, after studying village witch beliefs, conclude
that witches are only a form of the scapegoat that is always with us. See
Paul Bohannan, *op. cit.*, pp. 353–354; and Monica Hunter Wilson, "Witch
Beliefs and Social Structure," *The American Journal of Sociology*, LVI,
No. 4 (January 1951), 307–313.

whole fellowship that participates in psychic acts, mourns and shouts in tongues, dances after everyone else is in bed. The late hours of the Negro services have no small part to play in its fearsomeness.

A number of stories are also told about individual Negroes' powers. Thirty years ago a Negro man was hanged on a tree between Slide Hill Church and Applecross Store. An old stump stands there now, and the story goes that if you pass the stump at night on horseback the ghost of the Negro man drops down behind you and you feel him holding around your waist. Sometimes he rides up and down the road on a horse, and on the darkest nights you can see him hanging in the air above the stump.

"Free Julie" was a Negro slave who is said to have had strange powers to evade capture. She was strong and skilled and always welcome to hide out in Applecross to cook and sit with the sick, whom she doctored with herbs. Finally her master caught up with her. Because of her wandering, he put her on a sawed-off locust stump and sold her "under the hammer." She was taken southward to Florida, but according to our informant the stump still sings, "Won't see Julie no more; Julie's down the river."

The stigma related to racial deviation is plain. Important, too, to social control is the haunted stump found in both these stories. A hollow stump commonly contains either the whiskey bottle a distributor has left or the pay a consumer has left. For safety it should command respect from young and old, since hidden nearby many hollow stumps there is someone on sentry duty with eyes and gun fixed on the secret exchange.

A relation between witchcraft and the proscription against competition, or against excess accumulation of power and wealth, has been noted by Krige and Norbeck.[8] And in our

8. J. D. Krige, "The Social Function of Witchcraft," *Theoria: A Journal of Studies of the Arts Faculty, Natal University College* (1947), I, 8–21, and Edward Norbeck, *Religion in Primitive Society*, pp. 198–200.

community, too, it seems that men who have gone far in violating the valley's egalitarian norms, men who are considered dangerous socially because of an accumulation of education, property, or special skills, are the ones who curse and minister to those around them by supernatural means. This is true of one wealthy upper-Ridge resident who is in an important power position. His wife brags about his accomplishments but protects him from visitors. Neighbors say of him, "He can't scare me; I've known him always," but then admit there are ghosts on his hill and speak of him with fear and distrust.

Another man, with burning hatreds for his deceased father's enemies, lives closer to Big Rook. He is viewed as dangerously educated and an ill omen wherever he is seen. He "has known and still knows" every person buried in the five family graveyards around the open-country church. The graveyards are divided by aisles, and the church corner is a sort of meeting place for the families, many of whose deceased members were enemies. The man has a horror of riffraff and renegades being buried adjoining "worthy" family lines, and he tells neighbor and kin the "right" place to be buried. He keeps alive past conflicts between families; he also keeps alive blood-curdling Civil War events and believes it is time to reopen and settle the race issue, with another war if necessary. "I'd rather die nobly than disgraced," he says. Especially has he "put a curse" on one man in the area: "That yeller dog; his grandfather was a Yankee. If it hadn't of been for the Ku Klux Klan they'd of killed the South."

One valley kinsman who was deviant in that he achieved high status during World War I was described as "double breasted," that is, as having a double pair of lungs: "He wuz as thick through th' back as he wuz wide. You could hear him a mile away five minutes afore he died. He gave orders that were heard fur ten miles durin' combat."

Another educated upper-Ridge man has strange powers to grow and see things no one else can grow and see. He grows cabbages when the temperature is too cold for anyone else to grow them.[9] He has an eye that can see the intentions of men. There are large ticks in his fields "that'll go clean through one side of you and out th' other."

Still another kinsman has awesome encounters with Death, the concrete form of valley residents' greatest disappointment. He wears long black overcoats the year round, seemingly attempting to impersonate as well as describe his companion. His ability to foretell death he also claims for farm animals and says he gets some of his information by communicating with them. He has foretold the death of his parents and many of his neighbors. The Sunday before his wife became ill he saw her dressed in the black clothes of a corpse walking through a field in bright sunlight; then he saw her go into deep darkness and emerge again. He has also seen Death start toward him and then turn back. He discourages persons from visiting his sick wife. The lane approach to his home is overshadowed by a thick growth of tall trees, which any other valley resident fears to have growing close to his house.

These descriptions contain enough of the elements of witchcraft to draw several conclusions: Ridge residents' ideas of supernaturalism do indicate internal strains; there is structural significance in the objects, persons, and groups connected with supernatural stories; misfits, violators of valley norms, or the acquisitive invite suspicion—the same persons make use of their "powers" to secure a position in the community; and interpersonal relations continue on this basis with tensions somewhat relieved through the use of these community scapegoats.

Motives and Mores

So much for the evidences of tense relations and structural strain. Two important questions remain to be answered. What

9. Actually, he has a special Canadian cabbage over which he keeps a frame except when the sun shines, but this makes the unseasonal growing no less miraculous to everyone.

causes the strain? When the use of scapegoats, joking, or other release mechanisms fail, are there clear motives behind the violence that results?

Motives for killings are difficult to determine either by common talk or by news story or by court record (and the present analysis makes use of all three methods). Although one might argue that almost any interaction could be construed either as strengthening a collateral bond or as weakening threats to a collateral bond, this goal is stated explicitly in a number of violent incidents.

Examples of Ridge attempts to strengthen a collateral bond follow: A sixty-year-old farmer who lost his wife suddenly told neighbors he had nothing more for which to live and shot himself minutes later. A twenty-year-old farmer poured a can of lye in a well in an attempt to poison five of his wife's kin to "get even with 'em fur tryin' to separate me and my wife." Another farmer killed his mother-in-law and her son because they "were both more aggravatin' than you could stand." A man was killed in an attempt to defend his brother in a shooting fracas. Another was wounded while trying to protect a brother who was fatally shot after a dance. On the other hand, attempts at weakening the vertical bond are illustrated by a father who shot his son, another his daughter, and another his step-daughter during family arguments; two different men who committed suicide soon after going to live with their sons; a sixty-year-old man who killed his eighty-year-old uncle following an argument over some repairs to chicken feed troughs.

In the few cases of murders that do involve collateral kin, the after-effects appear very different from the after-effects of vertical killings. Slayer-slain identifications in Table 5 do not include the four newspaper cases of homicide followed by suicide (see Table 4). In three of these four cases a husband took his own life after killing his wife. The one incident of wife-killing that is listed in Table 5 was followed by attempted suicide on the part of the husband.

The only reported brother-killing occurred in 1959 when an older brother shot a younger one who was threatening to "kill the whole family." The paper states that he rushed to get medical help and then went voluntarily to the sheriff and confessed. This is not an attempt to explain away the conflict between the slayer-slain pairs having collateral ties, but remorse is more apparent in the cases of wife and brother murders.

The strength of collateral kinship ties and of far-reaching norms concerning strangers, higher education, or leaving the community, is demonstrated in such events as the following: Three murder victims were men who had moved away and then returned to live or visit. One lower-Ridge woman, in telling how her upper-Ridge brother killed his son-in-law, a "stranger" in the community, made several attempts at the victim's name: "————, ————, ————," she stumbled, "I never could say his name nohow." After an argument with her cousin about when their tobacco should be set, an upper-Ridge woman shot and was shot by the cousin, who then sat up all night with her even though he was suffering from severe wounds himself. An upper-Ridge girl who came from a family of fourteen children and was valedictorian of her high school committed suicide soon after graduation, leaving a note: "Sometimes I get so worried I cannot control myself. I have picked up a gun a number of times and put it back, but some day I may not put it back."

Why Violence?

The search for common grounds in outbursts of violence leads to some *ex post facto* causal interpretations of certain sociological factors. A number of these have been carried through the process of analytic induction. It seems appropriate to expound the most theoretically sound interpretations and to point out their relevance and deficiencies. This should clear the way for the last chapter of our book and for the hypothesis which, in the light of the substructures of our endogamous rural community, offers the most adequate explanation of strain.

First, the following explanation of violence appears feasible. In a community where no clear stratification system allocates scarce privileges and goods, where authorized power over persons and things tends to incur negative sanctions, confusion (sometimes leading to conflict) would likely accompany the distribution of desired resources. If a mate or if property is the highest valued article, the focus of the conflict is set.

This is seen in a number of tense situations dealing with marriage choice, with land transference, or with farm work-team decisions. The aggression may be against an opponent or it may be inward, resulting in suicide or self-banishment. In one case, a man's third cousin, who lived a mile away, refused to marry him. After the refusal the man shot himself, though not fatally, and the bridal choice gave her assent. In another case, a man in love with a woman whose husband was in a mental institution settled the complications of their courtship and marriage by taking her life and his in a nearby hollow. An uncle killed a niece with whom he was in love, her double first cousin who was dating her, and then himself; his widow left the valley. A lower-Ridge woman moved far away after she failed to get her mother's dowry. One man moved after arguing with and shooting five others over feeding cows.

Second, if persons are in constant interaction with others whom they have known long and well and whose approval or disapproval is of utmost importance, if there is little opportunity for avoiding one another through time and space— then intense feelings are bound to mount. It is in the complex, highly differentiated society that psychological devices such as displacement work best, for in such societies persons play more roles with more "others," facilitating the release of tensions in places and with persons apart from those causing the tensions. But where gradients of the love-hate, approval-disapproval dimensions are at stake, tense relations between those who are wholly and deeply and consistently involved may end in violence.

The release function of joking is evident at this point, especially between in-laws. The content of the jokes is revealing. In-law, Negro, and Church of Christ jokes are favorites; lower-Ridge residents tell terrible tales on upper-Ridge residents. The community misfits, members who have reputations of being miserly or greedy, the braggarts, or the sexually loose, are teased excessively. Mention has already been made of uncle-nephew joking relations and of joking between neighbors with differences. Joking is noticeable between those who are in danger of loving too much as well as too little. It is common between single first cousins of the opposite sex, between young couples who have always known and dated each other freely. Apparently many tensions and strains are legitimately alleviated through this means. The fact that north of Duck River Ridge are found more close-kin marriages and also more strain lends a priori support to the hypothesis that the more neighbor and kin and in-law coincide, the more intensive and danger-fraught is interaction.

Third, because of the general attitude toward interference from the outside, it is not surprising to find a self-help system in operation throughout the Ridge. Such a system is well integrated with an organization that rests on a moral order and has little basis in political authority. Ridge residents have a strong feeling against outside professional help. They prefer and use home veterinarians, home doctors, home preachers, home undertakers. In the past years a number of regular valley preachers and almost all of the summer revival preachers have been Ridge kinsfolk—an unusual practice for town and city churches and one which is considered unwise by high church officials. Most residents are horrified by the idea of being taken to hospitals, many of them exacting promises from kin that they will be allowed to die at home. They want "Doc _____" to treat them at home or in his county-seat office because they have "plowed many a day with him barefoot." A large percentage of the funerals of the valley are conducted from the home or at the family graveyard without the use of an undertaker. The favorite undertaker, when one is called, is a man who grew up in the valley and now lives about ten miles away.

In the institution of self-help, it is difficult to establish the point at which self-help, resistance to outside help, and crime overlap. Killings and injustices in a self-help system are not typically followed by institutionalized feuds or reprisal from the victims' kin.[10] Support in personal disagreements with kin or in-law or neighbor cannot be expected from larger valley groups. Kin and loyalty lines in a bilateral endogamous society are so interwoven that no one group can avenge another. There are no exclusive divisions to act as units.[11] For example, there was recently much talk over some marriage infidelities, such open discussions undoubtedly being important in social control. All talk ended with: "Well, it's bad, but I can't afford to do nothin'; I'm close kin to all of them."

For the same reason that the individual usually decides and acts alone, his aggression, though it means death to its victim, usually goes unavenged, and in many cases none will file suit or testify against him.[12] This is the bilateral endogamous community's demonstration of the unity of kindred, for in a pure sense each resident is being loyal to his genealogical set, which coincides with his community.[13]

Fourth, violence makes use of an ever-available means to

10. Paul Bohannan, *Justice and Judgment Among the Tiv*, pp. 146, 149.

11. George P. Murdock, *Social Structure*, pp. 60–61.

12. During the study a number of persons in neighboring Ridge communities commented that the Hancock case, a notorious East Tennessee murder in which no jury could be obtained, was no worse than certain Big Rook killings against which no one was willing to testify. See the *Nashville Banner*, June 4, 1962.

13. The fact that kin and community merge helps explain why both seem at times to take second place to the neighbor relation.

valley families, for most households are supplied with several loaded .22-caliber rifles and 12-gauge shotguns, and many also have .38-caliber pistols. Above the Ridge one sees more guns hanging over the doors or leaning against the walls. Rifles are used in killing woodchucks, hogs, and goats out in the pasture. Warning shots for stills are also fired from .22-caliber rifles. Pistols and shotguns are used more by the women for keeping varmints out of the garden. The shotgun is considered a special woman's weapon. Trading and showing guns is a favorite pastime above the Ridge. A Big Rook nine-year-old boy proudly showed the writer his first rifle, for which he had traded two pigs. Also, if one is to believe the county news, which usually manages to report that legal violators have been drinking—an issue probably kept alive because of the long history of moonshine through the area—the availability and consumption of liquor may be a violence factor in releasing normal inhibitions.

The fact that violence is predominantly an upper-Ridge phenomenon makes it impossible to accept any of the four conditions stated in this section as necessary and sufficient to produce excessive structural strain. It may be that the reader, with descriptive sections of family and community behind him, has already dismissed some of these hypotheses as not fitting our data.

The first one, dealing with the distribution of desired resources, is not adequate because less strain occurs below the Ridge where status distinctions are held more to a minimum. For the upper-Ridge and lower-Ridge populations, the amount of violence varies directly rather than inversely with the degree of stratification. We cannot attribute violence, then, to the absence of a clear system for allocating goods and privileges.

The second explanation is the interaction hypothesis. It is true that kin and in-law and neighbor more often coincide above the Ridge, but there is far more daily interaction among them below the Ridge. Upper-Ridge families more often leave the community for work, shopping, visitation, and club activities; they have, therefore, more opportunities to use the psychological displacement devices than do lower-Ridge families. The second hypothesis is hardly adequate.

Again, for the self-help hypothesis, data are in the wrong direction. Upper-Ridge residents have more connection with outside help, with the county seat, and with political authority than do lower-Ridge families. Wronged men above the Ridge actually do not need to take matters in their own hands as much as wronged men below the Ridge where there is a minimum of titles, leaders, and hierarchy. It is among the relatively undifferentiated that self-help patterns have been notorious.[14]

Therefore, even though we may contend that these three hypotheses point to violence-relevant conditions, or that they have validity in relation to other social theory, we have yet to explain why lower-Ridge territory is free of violence.

The availability of guns and liquor was mentioned as a fourth possible factor. More important than whether a person has ready access to a tool of violence or to the means of releasing normal inhibitions, however, is the absence or weakness of sanctions against violent offenses. In rating the degree of wrongness of certain acts, upper-Ridge residents more often named "fighting with one's neighbors" as the "most wrong." Yet the circuit court records are filled with fighting charges against upper-Ridge ladies (as well as men), whom ministers describe as "outstanding, kind, and sober Christians." Here is a vast distinction between ideal and actual behavior. Above many Big Rook mantels, shotguns hang side by side with placques that bear such a message as "Let us live together and love one another." As one man replied to the comment that Big Rook persons seemed very nice, "Yeah, they'll love ye and shoot ye and bury ye and no one will ever know."

14. Bohannan, *op. cit.*, pp. 8–9, 137–146.

Though some or all of these four factors may be related to violent acts, none is an acceptable explanation, for none accounts for the fact that violence occurs above, but not below, the Ridge. There will be an advantage in delaying our explanation of violence until the final chapter. This will allow us to focus on some theoretical insights which have grown out of our study so far—exciting formulations dealing with the pervading and significant So-So values, with sibling and other solidarity in the bilateral kinship system, and with certain other important exigencies of the deme, our structural type.

Part III. EVALUATION

9. Endogamy, Consolidation, and the Double Bond

THE deme is, by definition, endogamous and bilateral, a residential unit of intermarrying kindred composed of both parents' relatives. Membership within it is based on locality and blood ties. The deme discriminates among the total number of kinsfolk by distinguishing between those whose ancestors have remained over a number of generations on some original tract of land and those who have moved away.

Given bilateral kin and endogamy, alliances between families strengthen community solidarity. Exchanges of men are as vital as exchanges of women for this solidarity, and exchanges are for work as well as marriage alliances. In a sense a "new" family or a "new" work-team is never really formed, but there are merely rearrangements of members within a close corporate group of households.

Endogamy contributes to solidarity by serving important consolidating functions for the deme. Marrying endogamously means that family ties which would in time dissipate themselves are brought together through marriage relationship in one generation and through blood relationship in the next, giving continuity to kinship recognition and devotion. The intermarriage of cousins constantly consolidates kinsfolk as well as family farms. As has been emphasized in the case of the Iban or Sea Dyaks of Sarawak, one of the most important features of cousin marriages for a society is their reinforcement of the network of kinship ties.[1]

In the nonendogamous American community, meaningless proportions of kin accumulate. For example, if for the current and preceding generation the average number of children per completed family is 3, for the third ascending generation 6, and for the fourth ascending generation 8, and if all the sibling groups in each generation have descendants accordingly, then today's young person has 12 first cousins, 24 first cousins once removed, 72 second cousins, 144 second cousins once removed, more than 3,000 third cousins, and more than 50,000 fourth cousins. It is highly unlikely that a family has meaningful kinship relations with all the first and second cousins, and it is inconceivable that even the names of all third and fourth cousins are known. In a deme, however, close or vital kinship roles regularly displace distant or peripheral ones, take priority in recognition, and simplify and intensify relations. The duo-parental affiliations in a bilateral descent system that are in danger of becoming so numerous they lose their significance are reduced to significant numbers.[2]

Numerous meaningless affiliations are evident in the case of C and L, neighbors who stated sociometric preferences for each other as working companions. Diagrammed, their relations are clear, but these men do not recognize any kinship whatsoever. Actually, they are second cousins once removed through H and H' and third cousins once removed through A and A', who made first-cousin marriages with H and H'. When the children of C and L marry, close affinal ties will take precedence over distant consanguinal ones.

Typically, recognition of kin is greater for women than for men, and women generally talk more of kin ties. One wife became interested in her family lines and discovered her great-

1. J. D. Freeman, "The Iban of Western Borneo" in *Social Structure in Southeast Asia,* ed. George P. Murdock, pp. 65–88.

2. George P. Murdock, *Social Structure,* p. 44.

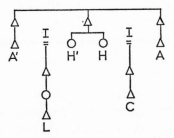

FIG. 16—*An unrecognized kin affiliation.*

grandmother was a Huntly. When she told her husband he was shocked: "I sure didn't know it, or I wouldn't have married you." "To heck with it," she said, "you're one too." His mother's mother and his mother's father's mother were both Huntlys.

The reader may recall that the deceased husband in the old homestead was two generations, and his wife three generations, removed from the Huntly sibship which they shared. In his case the relation was known; in hers it was not. With most Applecross residents, these are the distances crucial to recognition of descent lines. Most persons know their grandmothers' but not their great-grandmothers' maiden names, probably due in part to the fact that they usually have some face-to-face contact with their grandparents' siblings but none with their great-grandparents' siblings, in part to the fact that they have neither the time nor the affective energy to identify with eight ancestral lines, and in part to the primacy of collateral bonds which put secondary emphasis on descent lines.

The rejoining of kinship networks each third or fourth generation, therefore, is important for the deme in strengthening devotion and jealous regard for one another. It is important for the individual in simplifying and making meaningful the kin connections of those with whom he is in daily

contact. It is important for the family in combining and con-
serving economic assets.[3]

All three consolidating functions of endogamy are evident
in the theoretically significant alliance, the double bond (see
Chapter Four). We are ready now to explain the close
affective and instrumental ties between valley siblings and
cousins, why collaterals often stand together in choosing marriage partners from the same group of siblings, and why the
most cherished kinship relations require complex genealogical
charts. The explanation proceeds from a simple principle.

Bilateral systems are much more complicated than unilateral systems in that both parents' lines are viewed as important. This is why social anthropology has made more
progress in determining unilateral kinship principles. The very
root of a bilateral system's complexity furnishes the simple
but fundamental principle which we observed earlier. The
double bond, a kinship bond involving both parents, is the
tie of greatest conceivable value in a bilateral system.

The double bond is the basis of the close sibling relations
of a bilateral society, for a person is directly joined to his
siblings through the combined blood lines of father and
mother. Given this fact, it is no wonder that Codere and
Pehrson see the sibling bond as the main kinship feature of
the United States.[4] No wonder, too, that we find the rural
ideal of brothers in one family marrying sisters in another,
and the rural adage that double first cousins are closer than
brothers and sisters; only with the three basic double bonds—
double first cousin, full sibling, or half sibling where the

3. There are many instances outside of our deme in which endogamy
has served to consolidate economic assets. The wealthiest family in the
world today, the Rothschilds, has had a long history of first-cousin marriages in order not to waste its name or its fortune on "strangers." See
Frederic Morton, *The Rothschilds.*

4. Helen Codere, "A Genealogical Study of Kinship in the United
States," *Psychiatry,* XVIII (1955), 65–80, and Robert N. Pehrson,
"Bilateral Kin Groupings as a Structural Type," *Journal of East Asiatic
Studies,* III, No. 2 (January 1954), 199–203.

unshared parents are siblings—can one share identical sets of valuable bilateral kindred.

Neither is it surprising that in an endogamous bilateral community there are strong collateral ties making for an exceptionally close-knit deme; valley cousins, like siblings, are highly esteemed because they represent connections through both parents. One of the common remarks concerning Ridge cousins is, "He's kin to me on my mother's side and on my father's too."

The cohesion supplied by double ties is an important factor contributing to the low incidence of divorce in a deme. This is supported by the finding that, for twenty-eight bilateral societies, low divorce rates are associated with community endogamy and with consanguine endogamy (that is, when marriage is within the community and among the blood kin), the association being stronger when the two endogamy indices are combined.[5] The same cohesion supplies solidarity in cases of the sororate or levirate, the practices of marrying one's wife's sister or one's husband's brother. Furthermore, if a couple is older and the wife dies, it appears to be legitimate and "good" for the man and his deceased wife's sister to live together without marriage. And if there have been multiple marriages involved among the sibling groups, the probability of such an arrangement is maximized. For example, a widow moved to the house of her sister's husband to take care of him after his wife died. A niece explained that the elderly man was no blood kin to them but that he seemed especially close because "he and his brother married two of my mother's sisters."

Proceeding from the basic double bonds of siblings and double first cousins, many other double bonds are important in an endogamous community. We described and diagrammed a number of these in Chapter Four. It is clear that in a bi-

5. Charles Ackerman, "Affiliations: Structural Determinants of Differential Divorce Rates," *The American Journal of Sociology*, LXIX, No. 1 (July 1963), 13–20.

lateral system the double kinship ties give closer unity than could possibly come through ties with only one parent.

In the judgment of the writer, the implications of the double bond in a bilateral system provide the most significant theoretical insights of our study.

10. Some Particularistic-Ascriptive Patterns

WE have discussed one of the deme's characteristics, endogamy, and have seen its consolidating functions illustrated in the double bond. The deme as a type of particularistic-ascriptive community has certain other exigencies. Let us review those predicted by Parsons and confirmed by our data.[1]

Ascriptive cues to status—such as age, sex, membership in a kin group—are preferred over others. External relations are accepted only as they promote stability and order within the community; otherwise they are ignored. Emphasis rests on local creativity and on expressive acts such as singing and talking and handicrafts. The community is individualistic. There are no community "projects," no formal associations organized for special ends through collective activity. In church, home, or store expressive interaction has primacy and performance has no great social value. Excessive crying, loving, aggression appear inherent in the system.

Work is considered a routine and necessary activity. Productivity and profit are disvalued. Innovations, new crops, new methods are not sought. Immoral acts are viewed more as disruptive or "not done" than as bad. Just as a person works because he "needs to," he upholds a moral code because he "was raised up to it." Internal stability depends on this high elaboration of symbolic expressions.

The joining of these characteristics with a number of related

1. Talcott Parsons, *The Social System*, pp. 198–199.

propositions suggests certain structural effects for our deme.

Bennett and Despres delineate two types of kinship systems, reciprocal and nonreciprocal, according to the relation of traditional symbols or meanings to task performance or goal pursuit.[2] A system is reciprocal if at the same time that kinship rules and values are used to organize instrumental activities cultural continuity is reinforced by the pursuit of those activities. It is nonreciprocal if the culture is exploited to organize instrumental activities, as in a "boss-henchman" work-group in which ritualistic use of simulated kin ties serves managerial objectives. The corresponding states of the social system are logically traditional organization and rational organization.[3]

The Bennett-Despres typology is specific to kinship but otherwise proposes the same problems of integration as Merton's normative and social structures, Parsons's cultural and social systems, Homans's internal and external aspects of a system, or Kerckhoff's cultural expectations and social limitations.[4]

Integration is never complete in any social system, but it is approached through institutionalizing certain dominant values into roles. The kinds of values which are institutionalized affect the structural qualities of the roles and the state of the system as a whole. The father-provider role, for example, when influenced by achievement rather than ascriptive values, has norms that provide for more behavior outside the group and requires more role playing with different "others"

2. John W. Bennett and Leo B. Despres, "Kinship and Instrumental Activities: A Theoretical Inquiry," *American Anthropologist*, LXII, No. 2 (April 1960), 254–268.

3. Max Weber, *The Theory of Social and Economic Organization*, trans. A. M. Henderson and Talcott Parsons, ed. Talcott Parsons, Part I, pp. 112–123.

4. Robert K. Merton, *Social Theory and Social Structure*, pp. 161–164; Parsons, *op. cit.*, p. 5; George Homans, *The Human Group*, pp. 90–91; Alan C. Kerckhoff, "Some Contributions to the Social Systems Analysis of the Family," paper read before the twenty-fifth annual meeting of the Southern Sociological Association, Louisville, Kentucky, April 1962.

and in different institutions. Bates labels roles that call for
behavior outside the group as "extramural" rather than "intramural" and he labels roles that require interaction with
multiple persons as "distal" rather than "proximal." [5] Bates's
hypothesis is that there can be greater inconsistency between
roles which are extramural and distal without producing
serious conflict for the system.

Where a community has mostly intramural roles, that is,
where role requirements can be met within the group, and
where roles are proximal, that is, where they are played largely
with the same persons and in the same institutional framework, the structure is "tight," [6] both because of the connected
internal role system and because of the severe consequences
for the community should proximal roles have seriously con-
flicting expectations. Roles in such a community tend to be
diffuse, that is, played with regard to the total personalities
involved. Conversely, societies capable of tolerating a wide
diversity of behavior patterns must have norms related to
specific performances or single positions, that is, involving
only a segment of a total personality.[7]

The kinship unit is the unit that makes primary provisions
for the learning of roles and for the articulation of consti-
tuent human parts within the social system. Solidarity of that
unit is, at some level, imperative for every society.[8] A search
for the basis of kinship solidarity leads us to another structural effect.

Cumming and Schneider postulate a difference between

5. F. L. Bates, "Some Observations Concerning the Structural Aspect
of Role Conflict," paper read before the twenty-fifth annual meeting
of the Southern Sociological Association, Louisville, Kentucky, April 1962.

6. A tight structure is one in which behavior conforms closely to formal
social patterns with very little individual deviation. See John F. Embree,
"Thailand, a Loosely-Structured System," *American Anthropologist*, LII
(April-June 1950), 181–186.

7. John Mogey, "Introduction," *International Journal of Comparative
Sociology*, III, No. 2 (September 1962), 4.

8. Talcott Parsons, "An Outline of the Social System" in *Theories of
Society*, ed. Talcott Parsons, *et al.*, I, 47–48, 59.

horizontal solidarity (cohesion between siblings and other collaterals) and vertical solidarity (cohesion between descendants and ascendants). In vertical solidarity there is dissimilarity accompanying the division of labor, mutual dependency, and obligation. In horizontal solidarity units are similar but are not dependent on one another, and sociability is predominant.[9]

Vertical or lineal kin thus exhibit instrumental orientation, while collateral or horizontal kin show expressive interests.[10] Kinship solidarity is organized, in the one instance, around collective morality and the lineage group; in the other it is organized around individual morality and the sibling group.

The dimensions are also useful in other theory. For example, the Protestant movement rests on horizontal solidarity and the Roman Catholic on vertical. Protestants make their appeal through Christ, the fellow-sufferer, the expressive elder brother, and usually refer to their minister or another church member as "brother" or "sister." Catholics, on the other hand, have a lineal appeal: the mother Mary, the instrumental Father, the name of "father" for popes and priests, and the traditional laying on of hands. Here, too, there is a close link between the individual morality and horizontal solidarity of Protestants and between collective morality and vertical solidarity of Catholics. Indeed, we may ask whether the spread of Christianity in the first centuries was due in part to the appeal of a new covenant of brotherhood and of commensalistic patterns among newly arrived urban peoples isolated from a familiar sibling social order.

9. Elaine Cumming and David M. Schneider, "Sibling Solidarity: A Property of American Kinship," *American Anthropologist*, LXIII, No. 3 (June 1961), 505.

10. According to Parsons, where most instrumental functions are performed in kinship roles there may be a fusion of expressive and instrumental orientations. Our deme's vertical relations tend to be instrumental only, whereas its collateral relations are both expressive and instrumental. See Talcott Parsons, *The Social System*, pp. 157–158, 175–176.

Radcliffe-Brown's unity of the sibling group and unity of alternate generations are both functions of the relation between affectivity and horizontal solidarity, the grandparent-grandchild bond having the same qualities as the sibling bond.[11] That instrumental parent-child accents give way to expressive ones not only between horizontal or collateral kin but also in contacts between alternate generations, is evident in such statements as, "I was too busy to enjoy my own children, but I just *love* my grandchildren—don't even try to make them mind." These dimensions also shed light on why distance between a man and his wife's parents is maintained by avoidance or instrumental acts such as sending gifts or laboring for them, while distance between a man and his wife's siblings is maintained by bantering and joking.[12]

According to Table 6, then, our community is traditional, tight, showing horizontal solidarity. In other words, it is organized around reciprocal relations between culture and activity, close proximity of primarily intramural roles, and predominantly individual morality. The reciprocity between culture and activity in our community is seen in the reinforcement between stated ideals and actual patterns of education, leadership, participation, marriage and residence choices. It is seen too in such practices as endogamy and the formation of double bonds through multiple alliances, for these activity patterns have firm bases in the kinship culture and, in turn, give stability to that culture. Tightness of structure in our community is evident in the consistency of participants' expectations and values, their conformity to norms, diffuse role orientations, and connected interaction networks. Individual rather than collective morality is manifested in a strong hori-

11. Is it possible that the affective relation between alternate generations is necessary for intergenerational solidarity? See A. R. Radcliffe-Brown and Daryl Forde, *African Systems of Kinship and Marriage,* pp. 29–30.

12. A. R. Radcliffe-Brown, *Structure and Function in Primitive Society,* p. 90.

TABLE 6

Structural Aspects of Kinship Networks Applied to Parsons's Four Ideal Type Societies

Internal Relations	Intervening Factor	Consequent State of System	Societal Types and Examples			
			Univ.-Ach. (Industrial U.S.A.)	Univ. Asc. (Nazi Germany)	Part.-Ach. (Classical China)	Part.-Asc. (Our Deme)
Reciprocity between Culture and Activity	Instrumental Activity Reinforcing and Stabilizing Norms	Traditional Organization			x	
Nonreciprocity of Culture and Activity	Symbols Being Exploited for the Instrumental Goals (Bennett and Despres, 1960)	Rational Organization (Weber, 1947)	x			
Close Role Proximity	Diffuse Performances Necessitating Consistency, Conformity	Tight Structure		x	x	x

	Loose Structure (Embree, 1950)	Horizontal Solidarity	Vertical Solidarity (Cumming and Schneider, 1961)
High Role Distance (Bates, 1962)	x		
Specific Performances Encouraging Diversity in Behavior (Mogey, 1962)			x
Individual Morality — Dependency on Mutual Aid Ideally Absent, Expressions of Sociability and Affection Present (Embree, 1950)	x		
Collective Morality — Mutual Dependence, Help Patterns, Instrumental Activity Underlying Group Cohesion (Parsons, 1951)		x	x

Note: The above table attempts to relate six general states of the social system to the internal and intervening factors which are held at least in part responsible for these states and to classify Parsons's four ideal types of societies (please see footnote 11 in Introduction) along these dimensions. The table concerns broad organizational outcomes of limitations placed on societies through varying dominance of, and varying institutionalized forms of, kinship norms and values. It will be recognized that these dimensions overlap, but the value of such a table lies in the effort to determine just what relations lead one society to be rationally organized and tight and another to be traditionally organized and tight, or just what conditions result in a concurrence of traditionalism and horizontal solidarity for one society but rationalism and horizontal solidarity for another.

zontal solidarity, in which sociability and affection loom more important in the minds of the kinsfolk than giving and receiving instrumental aid.

Confusion may be avoided by stating again that the individualism of our deme involves expressive interests rather than performance or achievement. Such individualism is not in conflict with a tight structure or with strict conformity to traditional community values, but rather is opposed to collective programs and planning. As can be seen in Table 6, individual morality is found along with a loose structure in industrial America (the universalistic-achievement type); in that case the individualism is concomitant with ambition, achievement, and diversity of behavior.

11. Social System Control and the Egalitarian Ideal

STRUCTURAL-FUNCTIONAL analysis rests on the concept of certain control mechanisms at work within the social system—the perpetuation of structure through institutionalization and internalization of norms; the orientation of goals; the adaptation [1] required for goal attainment; and, central to sociology, the integration of each boundary-maintaining unit with the system as a whole. These four imperative functions of any system are pattern-maintenance, goal-attainment, adaptation, and integration.[2]

Data from this study suggest the following clustering of these control mechanisms: given consensus of goals only on a community level, plus integration on the basis of mechanical solidarity or the cohesion of likes,[3] a society has adaptation without stratification, and latent pattern maintenance is based on an ascribed status system with very little ambition or acquisitiveness. By contrast, our knowledge of metropolitan U.S.A. suggests that when goal consensus involves a structure in addition to or besides the community, and when solidarity stems from a high division of labor, a society has adaptation with stratification, an achieved status system, and the personal ambition which goes along with these. Applecross-Millstone

1. Adaptation involves the adopting of certain patterns in the process of adjusting the existing conditions of a system to goals of the system.

2. Talcott Parsons, "An Outline of the Social System" in *Theories of Society*, ed. Talcott Parsons, *et al.*, I, 60–70.

3. Emile Durkheim, *The Division of Labor in Society*, trans. George Simpson, pp. 70–71.

clearly exhibits the first group of characteristics, but Turnabout Hollow is not so easily typed.

TABLE 7

Clusterings of Control Mechanisms

	Applecross-Millstone	Metropolitan U.S.A.
Goal Attainment	community level	other-than-community level
Integration	mechanical solidarity	organic solidarity
Adaptation	without stratification	with stratification
Latent Pattern Maintenance	ascriptive basis	achievement basis

Mechanical solidarity is at its maximum when the group conscience coincides at all points with the individual conscience.[4] This accounts for the nonleadership situation in Applecross-Millstone. Since an informal leader is one who adheres closely to all the norms, and ideally in a community bound by mechanical solidarity all members adhere to all the norms, there is no need for informal leaders. Furthermore, in Applecross-Millstone, since goal consensus does not involve a level other than the community itself, there is no need for a representative leader. In fact, a representative leader's role demands adherence to larger societal norms as well as those of the community and, consequently, membership in a stratified system. Such a resident divorces himself from the deme.

Even though the condition was anticipated on some levels, the most surprising discovery of this study is the degree to which Ridge families, especially in Applecross-Millstone, succeed in keeping stratification to a minimum. We had a second surprise: we made little progress in explaining upper-Ridge violence because of our failure to explain Applecross-Millstone's lack of violence. Our primary task, as suggested in

4. *Ibid.*, p. 130.

Chapter Eight, is to analyze the high cohesion of Applecross-Millstone.[5]

The reader may recall the observation of a man who was born in Applecross and now lives several miles away: "The community is different from any other place; people there are all just the same. No one wants to get ahead of anyone else. No one is up high where others think he's high." What is this pervading theme around which the deme organizes its activities? Having the common occupation of farming, having approximately the same amount of land, of equipment, of formal and informal learning, marrying endogamously so that statuses seldom vary, these kinsfolk support by words and activity an ideology which breaks down distinctions among them.

It seems to the writer that one of the major goals held out before the deme is that of making uniform the life chances, or the opportunities and risks, of its members. Unlike many efficiency-minded Americans who point to the amount of time "wasted" in rural neighbor and community relations, Eric Wolf sees social relations in his peasant communities as long-time life insurance.[6] He explains certain practices in terms of lessening the threats that endanger the pattern of equal distribution of risks developed over a period of time by the community members. For example, community endogamy limits the influx of new people which might upset the system by decreasing the amount of land available to community members; similarly, to prevent decrease in size of farms, surplus population is pushed off into other villages.

5. If we follow Marxist theory, violence is the thesis and harmony the antithesis, strain is a function of the incompatibility between social and normative structures, and the substratum of conflict demands less explanation than the condition of order. See Georg Simmel, *Conflict*, trans. Kurt H. Wolff, pp. 13–20; also David Lockwood, "Some Remarks on 'The Social System,'" *British Journal of Sociology*, VII (June 1956), 134–146.

6. Eric R. Wolf, "Closed Corporate Peasant Communities in Mesoamerica and Central Java," *Southwestern Journal of Anthropology*, XIII (1957), 1–19.

Surplus wealth is viewed with hostility, for it could alter the balance of land in favor of the families who accumulate it. Community membership and the purchase of land are restricted to those born and raised within the community boundaries. Cultural alternatives are excluded through autonomous economic, social, and political systems.[7] Though these descriptions are for closed, corporate communities in Mesoamerica and Central Java, they fit equally the Applecross-Millstone deme.

In the chapter on values, we discussed a number of factors related to status that are frowned upon by the deme: ambition, leadership, higher formal education, material acquisitiveness. We referred to this as a nonsuccess ideology. In the light of such a noncompetitive, egalitarian ideal, many of the So-So substructures become meaningful, for much Applecross-Millstone activity serves a status-equalizing function. The deme's control through auctions, along with its efforts to see that land and equipment go to those who need them, has a leveling function. In general and especially in Applecross-Millstone, residents prefer to have the same equipment, even the same mixed breed of animals as their neighbors. In this light too education data make sense. Residents prefer not to get more education than those around them; thus a number of young people drop out of high school just before finishing. Persons who have excess education and possessions leave the community. Persons who buy too many "knick-knacks" or are too ambitious are criticized.

The "Miss Abbie" ideal, revealed in community conversation even more than in sociometric choices, can be analyzed as part of the larger egalitarian ideology. A group's sociometric choice of the quiet, unassuming, well-dressed person who audibly contributes very little has been found in other situations in which there is pulling away from leadership.[8]

7. *Ibid.*, p. 5.

8. John Mogey, "The Climate of Opinion on Housing Estates," *The Sociological Review*, IV, No. 1 (July 1956), 74.

Also in the light of these ideals, swapping out arrangements take on new meaning. In fact, all of the collateral residence and work patterns of Applecross-Millstone involve fewer status distinctions than do lineal relationships, which from the start have more built-in ascriptive differences. The So-So ideals, especially strong in Applecross-Millstone, are institutionalized into many activity patterns which, in turn, support the egalitarian goals. This support is aided by a system of endogamous marriages and minimum external boundary penetration for county, state, or national purposes. Thus we see a strong complementary relationship between egalitarian goals and the leveling processes used in attaining them.

Social control among Applecross-Millstone neighbor and kin is rooted in such structural exigencies as were discussed in the preceding chapter—the reinforcement between actual and ideal behavior, behavioral conformity due to tight boundary maintenance, and individual morality expressed through collateral kinship bonds. In other words, integration in Applecross-Millstone follows the inherent congruity of the control mechanisms in operation.

We are now ready to analyze excessive structural strain above Duck River Ridge in terms of our knowledge of certain egalitarian ideals, of the social control mechanisms at work in our deme, and of the characteristics of an endogamous bilateral community.

12. An Explanation of Strain

HERE is an intriguing paradox of the deme-type structure: at what point do the strong and integrating kinship ties become forces of destruction, and what structural deficiencies can distort a peace-loving affective system into a desperately violent one? One resident colorfully defined the upper-Ridge situation: "It's the best place in all the world to live. Never was friendlier, nicer folks. Nothin' ever happens to strangers. But jest among the folks livin' here sometimes, and fur as long as anyone can remember, there'll be a full-scale war, people get slaughtered, and then the next day you'd never know what happened." Apparently a fighting community and a friendly community are only a step away from each other.

One of the surest things to say about Turnabout Hollow and other upper-Ridge violence is that it is endemic. It has a long history. It is a steady state in a stable system and thus cannot be attributed to technical, political, or social change. As one of the long-standing evidences of strain, violence itself points to the area's capacity to resist change. Rather than the lower-Ridge epigram "Leave us alone to enjoy ourselves in peace," [1] the upper-Ridge epigram should read, "Leave us alone to continue our violence." This is the same condition that has been identified in India, Jamaica, and New Mexico. Siegel and Beals call it "pervasive factionalism" and say that

1. W. J. H. Sprott, "Principia Sociologica," *The British Journal of Sociology,* III, No. 3 (September 1952), 203–221.

it by no means implies an unstable society, but that rather in the face of powerful pressures, such societies have unusual self-maintenance capacity.[2] The explanation of violence must be based on internal analyses.

Let us return to the internal control mechanisms of goal-attainment and adaptation. In the process of reducing discrepancy between the needs of a system and environing conditions, certain patterns are adopted; these patterns themselves become goal-directed. This is what Allport means by "functional autonomy of motives." [3] Adaptations become goals after meeting system needs, whether the system needs are or are not still present.

The pervading goal of our deme is leveling life chances and life risks, and the internal adaptive process is status equalization. These are the So-So patterns. They are both goals and adaptations, and they are maintained through high individual investment in social relations. They are most effective when they are on the community level and when they engage collateral kinsfolk.

The first condition for effectiveness means that underlying egalitarian norms are best supported in a closed corporate community, that is, in a cohesive community which draws its boundaries tightly against the "outside world." Such a community is composed of families which keep their doors and lives open to one another, and within these families men and woman are likely to perform separate tasks rather than to work jointly at the same jobs.[4]

2. Bernard Siegel and Alan R. Beals, "Pervasive Factionalism," *American Anthropologist*, LXII, No. 3 (June 1960), 394–417.

3. G. W. Allport, *Personality, A Psychological Interpretation*, pp. 190–212.

4. The positive relation between strictly segregated marital roles, nuclear families that are highly interconnected and open to one another, and a community that is closed to outside influences has been documented by Saal and Bott. In contrast, when a community boundary is open the family boundaries are usually closed, and spouses largely practice joint-role relations. See C. D. Saal, "Causes of the Delay in Western European

In brief, carrying out egalitarian norms necessitates a closed community made up of open families practicing segregated marital role relations. These factors are especially evident in Applecross-Millstone. Husband-wife duties are well differentiated. A free, unrestrained interaction exists among families, along with well-defined and maintained community boundaries. There are very few institutions, and these are carefully controlled, for they are local extensions of the deme's norms and personnel. On the other hand, in Turnabout Hollow, joint roles are common: a wife and husband more often work at the same tasks. There is more of a closed-family system, some family groups being completely closed occupationally. Institutions are largely out of the deme's control. Turnabout Hollow is more segmented, spatially and socially. Community boundaries, being more open, are more often penetrated.

This says to sociologists once again that some division of labor is essential to any social system. The fundamental division, that of husband and wife, can lead to an otherwise unstratified community if a community's goal of equalizing life chances is unchallenged by goals on other levels, such as a vertically knit family system. And this brings us to a second condition for most effective leveling of members of a kinship community.

The norm of equivalence is best supported by a family structure based on the collateral bond. The collateral bond fosters mechanical solidarity by involving a kinship system which looks outward to the association of likes,[5] by maximizing affective orientation, and by discouraging vertical familial alliances that cut across community goals. When extended family lines develop as closed corporate groups, equal distribution of life chances and risks is impossible. Our two conditions,

Family Research and Some Notes of the Investigations of the Dutch Rural Family" in *Studies of the Family*, ed. Nels Anderson, I, pp. 229–245; also, Elizabeth Bott, *Family and Social Network*, pp. 52–97.

5. F. M. Keesing, *Cultural Anthropology*, p. 272.

needed to support egalitarian norms in a kinship community —open families and strong collateral relations—thus come together.[6]

In particular, in Turnabout Hollow, distinguishing factors are set against equalizing factors. Interfering with the corporate community's claim on resources are the claims of separate corporate family lines, knit by lineal bonds at the expense of collateral bonds and divided in their pursuit of resources. Rather than a territorial entity, such a system is the sum total of different families. This explains why Applecross-Millstone boundaries are easily identified geographically, but Turnabout Hollow and Big Rook are said to extend wherever certain family lines extend. It is related to the prevalence of neighbor work-teams below the Ridge and father-son work-teams above, to collateral residence patterns below and lineal residence patterns above. It is connected with the larger number of persons who return to Turnabout Hollow to live near parents. It also helps explain why above the Ridge, where property trespassing could threaten a corporate family's still operations, people take offense if they are asked the whereabouts and business of a neighbor; below the Ridge, residents delight in telling where their neighbors are and what they are doing.

We know that any system of stratification distributes the things that society produces, such as life chances or life styles, prestige or power or status or leadership. If a deme has control over privileges and goods it may wish to distribute them equally to all. In upper-Ridge territory, however, resources connected with moonshine activities are controlled by nuclear families and lineage groups. At the same time upper-Ridge residents maintain on a purely ideological basis the egalitarian goals of helping each other and of "holding together" as neighbors. Thus prestige is bifurcated between family lines

6. Violent attempts to strengthen collateral bonds or to weaken vertical bonds take on significance here. See Chapter Eight.

which share and family lines which control desired resources. This bifurcation explains why one Turnabout Hollow leader has very high esteem since he distributes or "shares" resources for consumption, while another leader is in very low esteem since he profits from controlling the means of production. The power conflict between these two leaders is indicative of the conflict throughout Turnabout Hollow between egalitarian community ideals on the one hand and lineage group loyalties and opportunities on the other.

The problem is an adaptive one between the So-So values and family-community organization. In Applecross-Millstone the two are congruent, but in Turnabout Hollow and Big Rook the goals and structure of the vertically knit families are antagonistic to the leveling goals of the community. Disharmony in Turnabout Hollow derives from the incompatibility of the Ridge-wide norms of neighbors helping each other, standing together, and sharing, with the actual practice of closed families looking out for themselves, being enterprising in economic processes outside the community, and acquiring wealth at the expense of other families. Harmony in Applecross-Millstone derives from the same norms supporting and being strengthened by collateral swapping-out practices, neighbor co-operation within a closed community, and an horizontally knit open-family system.

This theoretical explanation of deviant behavior suggests an opposite side to Robert Merton's classic theme. Where Merton sees delinquency and crime as growing out of the moral mandate to *achieve* success in the *absence* of institutionalized means, this study points to the mandate to *avoid* success in the *presence* of institutionalized means.[7] A nonsuccess ideology, incompatible with an existing economic structure, can produce strain as surely as a monetary success goal that is not accompanied by prescribed and legitimate methods of reaching it. Where ambition, leadership, educa-

7. Robert K. Merton, *Social Theory and Social Structure*, pp. 166–170.

tion, material surplus, and status symbols are regarded with disapproval, and where a society places high premium on equality, then strain is to be expected from adaptive processes that make some families more affluent than others.

Our finding likewise gives a reverse twist to Hyman Rodman's "value stretch." The value stretch is an alternative set of values developed by the lower class as a response to their deprived situations. Rodman sees these individuals as acquiring a taste for sour grapes because the sweet grapes are not available.[8] Sweet grapes *are* within the reach of upper-Ridge residents, but because of the So-So ideals, they leave a bad taste in the mouths of those who eat them.

8. Hyman Rodman, "The Lower-Class Value Stretch," *Social Forces*, XLII, No. 2 (December 1963), 205–216.

Concluding Note

Significance of the So-Sos

THE attempt to explain structure and strain in an egalitarian kinship community has called for focus on a way of life that is so early American that some may even call it anti-American. Others may argue that the So-So structure is of interest as a unique case in western society but that its significance stops there.

At the time this is being written numerous newspaper articles are being written about the concern over conditions, especially education, in the Appalachian regions. Some of the articles ask about the right to be different, even non-literate.

The So-Sos are literate, but they are different. They dislike government interference; they speak of communism as the greatest possible intrusion on human freedom and as unimaginably horrible. The So-Sos have an ideal of democratic autonomy which expects a government to foster freedom but with a minimum of interference. One of the important questions facing western democracies is how much the government should do for people against their will.

We contrasted So-So ideals to the success ideology of our time in the final explanation of violence. Professor John Mogey asks an interesting question: "Would the rest of the U.S.A. have a Go-Go culture? And would Go-Go norms intruding into Turnabout Hollow be the cause of violence?" Indeed, does not the intrusion of Go-Go families and ideals into any So-So community result in structural strain? The reverse does not occur however. That is, the intrusion of So-So families into a Go-Go society does not cause violence: it only leads to an enlarging of the lower strata of the Go-Go society; it makes for an egalitarian island that is ironically misunderstood in a modern democracy.

In terms both of the So-Sos' egalitarian ideals and also of their right to be let alone, it is interesting that Erich Fromm means by "escape from freedom" an escape from the freedom to pursue prestige, power, wealth, fame, and other success emblems.[1] There may be other widely different groups in our society who are making an effort to escape organized social movements, leadership, or dominant career orientations. For instance, what of the kind of permanent strike against these emphases on the part of Greenwich Village Beats?[2] Or what of the firm stand against work and authority taken by certain American motorcycle gangs? Or, closer, what do upwardly-mobile, middle-class businessmen mean by the statement, "I wish I could get out of the rat race"?

As one sociologist writes in a business journal, we are used to recognizing the problems of the man who does not successfully climb the business ladder; such a man must downgrade his expectations to fit his achievements. We have largely overlooked the problems of the "unsung hero," however, or the man who succeeds beyond his aspirations. Such a man often feels fearful and guilty. It is a "hapless man that succeeds too well."[3] Are there evidences of keeping "down" with the Joneses in parts of our society? What status-equalizing processes are at work in nonendogamous closed neighborhoods of America?

We have gone far with professionalization and institution-

---

1. Erich Fromm, *Escape from Freedom*, pp. 103–109.
2. Ned Polsky, "The Village Beat Scene: Summer, 1960," *Dissent*, VIII, No. 3 (1961), 339–359.
3. Wilbert E. Moore, "Three Views of the Businessman," *Duns' Review and Modern Industry*, LXXX, No. 6 (December 1962), 66.

alization in our day. One major Protestant denomination has recently placed more rigid professional requirements upon its rural ministers and has, for reasons of efficiency and administrative economy, consolidated and rearranged many of its rural churches and largely-rural districts. (One wonders whether efficiency and economy have become goals, rather that means, throughout our society.) According to the So-So ideals, well-paid and professionally oriented seminary men may be more instrumental in the death of egalitarian-structured rural churches than the removal of sanctuaries.

As vital parts of our kinship communities, how much autonomy should such institutions have? In particular, to what extent should rural schools and churches be required to meet certain standards or die? How long can the rural kinship community survive without them? How much respect is due the So-So values, whether they are found in isolated, homogeneous valleys of extended kin or among the members of a geographically and occupationally mobile family?

We have also gone far with the slogan that education is America's wisest investment. Is it conceivable that there are long-term dividends as great or greater from certain investments in kin and neighbor relations?

It is hardly the purpose of this book to answer such questions as the above even if complete answers were clear to the writer, and they are not. Some observations do remain clear: no society can be based entirely on achievement as a mechanism for allocation to roles. The kinship network is, by far, the most significant factor influencing role behavior patterns among the So-Sos. Kinship ideology undoubtedly also exerts its influence in metropolitan U.S.A. Whatever the structural complexity of a society, the unit of the kin group, the family, is for personalities the major point of entry into that society. Our inquiry deals with a few of the exciting explorations that lie ahead for persons interested in the kinship community.

Appendix, Bibliography, Index

Appendix

DATA COLLECTION AND RELIABILITY

THE accompanying questionnaire was designed to help give content to the study of roles and attitudes necessary for determining the characteristics of a particularistic-ascriptive community. Probably even more important for structural analysis are the extensive kinship charts and formal kinship information secured with each questionnaire. Additional data were collected through informal visits, participant observation, informants, newspapers, census, legal and other records, leading to a sizable amount of information on actual activity patterns and on normative attitudes and values.

No serious problems were encountered in obtaining data, although it is almost impossible for outsiders to gain access to some of the homes around Duck River Ridge because of the illegal character of moonshining and its prevalence in sections of the Tennessee Valley Divide. The writer's status as preacher's wife in a circuit of churches above and below the Ridge meant, for the most part, open doors to her and her husband. Their statuses undoubtedly channeled responses toward greater ideal than actual dimensions. This was especially evident in the minister's interviews. The limitation was balanced by intimate association with families and their activities.

As minister's wife, the investigator was a part of Ridge community life for twelve months before deciding to study the area. She and her family helped with tobacco planting and other farm activities in the valleys. Most of the sixty-four homes had already been visited, but during the summer months and early fall of 1962 they were revisited a number of times, both for specific information and for general familiarity with the field. Visits were also made to nine households of kinsfolk who have moved away from the valleys. There were many opportunities to participate in country store talk, auctions, singings, school and church functions. In the months of data collecting, approximately a hundred community gatherings were visited, 178 home visits were made in Turnabout Hollow and the adjoining Big Rook area, and 154 in Applecross-Millstone.

Questionnaires were completed for the sixty-two adults in Applecross-Millstone. Husbands and wives were interviewed simultaneously in separate rooms with answers recorded at the time of the visit. Less than two weeks elapsed between the first and last formal Applecross-Millstone interviews, but this schedule did not prevent some respondents from literally memorizing questions and stock answers. Often residents caught themselves in antithetical responses. There was good rapport between interviewers and interviewees in Applecross-Millstone.

In Turnabout Hollow, questionnaires were completed for twelve of the sixty adults before residents expressed unwillingness to answer mimeographed questions. Interviewers were met with, "You may come in if you don't ask questions," and "The less we know about each other the better." One Turnabout Hollow man said nothing in a thirty-minute visit but "yassuh" while his wife and grown children, who were "not at home," giggled behind a half-open door. Interviewers were refused admittance on two occasions and accused several times of being with the government. Turnabout Hollow visits were completed on an informal basis with partial answers secured in this manner. Since the most valuable information came from unscheduled contacts, missing written questionnaires were not perceived as a serious handicap to the analysis.

Neither was the planned use of informants as yielding as the voluntary comments and answers of each household group during unscheduled visitation rounds. Acting as informants were two older Turnabout Hollow couples, middle-aged couples in both Millstone and Applecross, and three nonresident couples. The nonresident informants included a ninety-year-old couple who once lived in Turnabout Hollow and now reside thirty miles away and two middle-aged couples living fifteen miles from the area but still active in valley social events.

There was satisfactory agreement in material obtained from multiple informants; moreover, internal factual reliability was good throughout the analysis. Kinship charts, duplicated from household to household, were checked against one another. A large volume of helpful supplementary material was accessible from county and state libraries, such as filed clippings, county newspapers dating back to 1814, Tennessee census sheets from 1820 to 1880, will and deed and marriage records, court trial records, and outdated rural delivery and geological maps. These were studied for external reliability along with historical, genealogical, and violence information secured from the present generation of deme members.

The most serious technical problems for the functional view used in this analysis concern validity. In the incongruity between patterns presumed to measure the same attributes, the validity problem is readily apparent. For example, questions 31 and 32 of the formal questionnaire are supposed to measure the expressive-instrumental dimension. The majority of respondents prefer just talking or singing to playing games (an expressive orientation), but they prefer a mate who is a real help to one who is loving (an instrumental orientation). Such variations are viewed in the light of structural imperatives and of other data. In this case, as suggested in Chapter Four, a helpful wife, like work, may be a necessary evil. It certainly appears that the "warm and loving" spouse is the valley norm. Construct validity is aided by the literature references in Chapter X, which help answer the question, "Are we measuring what we purport to measure?" along the broad organizational lines of Table 6.

Plans were revised upon realization that it would not be possible to employ statistical techniques in the ways first designed. The questionnaire had to be rewritten after a test run in Big Rook. Some hoped-for methodological offspring did not come from this union between sociology and social anthropology, but compensating were anomalous and serendipitous findings—those unexpected attendants that have often resulted from a study in depth of a single people and have made many original propositions look second best.

QUESTIONNAIRE

1. Name _____
2. Age ____
3. Occupation _____
   If farmer,
      how much land? _____
      how many stock? ____
      _____
4. Where did you go to school?
   Millstone ___ Fraserburgh ___
   Elsewhere _____
5. What grade did you go
               through? ____
6. Single _____ Married _____
   Divorced ___ Widowed ___
7. Where did you spend most
   time when growing up?
   This community _____
   Nearby _____
            (where?)
   Elsewhere _____
            (where?)
8. Church member? _____
   Which church? _____
9. Hold an office? _____
   What? _____
10. How often do you attend?
    _____
11. Are you a member of any
    other organization (such as
    Farmer's Asso., Home
    Dem.)? _____
    What? _____
12. Do you hold an office? ____
    What? _____

13. How often do you attend?
    _____
14. What was your age at first
    marriage? _____
    Your (spouse's) age? _____
    Year you married? _____
15. Did you and your (spouse)
    attend the same school? ___
16. Did you live in this com-
    munity immediately before
    marriage? _____
       Less than 10 miles away?
       _____
       More than 10 miles away?
       _____
17. How many traveling miles
    did you live from your
    (sponse)? _____
18. How long had you known
    one another when you mar-
    ried? _____
19. When you decided to marry,
    who was told first?
    _____
20. Who made arrangements
    for the wedding?
    _____
21. Right after marriage, where
    did you live?
       With your folks? _____
       With (spouse's) folks?
       _____
       Elsewhere? _____
            (where?)

22. Have you been married again? _____
    If so, to whom? _____
    How many traveling miles did you live from this (spouse)? _____

23. How did you come to live in this house? [Gift from own or (spouse's) parents, bought from own or (spouse's) parents, built by self, built it with help of others (kin, family, neighbors), hired it built, rent it, etc.]

    _____

    _____

24. During the past month or so, what kin in this community have you gotten together with, and what did you do together? (as parents, married children, brothers and sisters, aunts and uncles, nieces and nephews, grandparents and grandchildren, 1st, 2nd, 3rd cousins, great aunts and uncles, great nieces and nephews, in-laws)
    (Give name and relation of person, about how often seen, and the purpose of the get-together, as for advice, pure sociability, to borrow something, work together, go somewhere together, etc.)

25. Do you think people who are kin should be able to expect more of one another than friends or neighbors?

Here are about thirty questions to which there aren't any right or wrong answers. Just tell me the way you happen to feel about them.

26. Young people have been taking gasoline from you and getting into other mischief in the valley. You find out their names and that they live in Nashville, but you don't know their address. How would you handle this?
    Go to the law _____
    Handle it some other way

    _____
    (how?)

27. If they were children of your neighbors, how would you handle it?
    Go to the law _____
    Handle it some other way

    _____
    (how?)

28. If they were children of your close kin, how would you handle it?
    Go to the law _____
    Handle it some other way

    _____
    (how?)

29. Would you prefer your neighbors to take care of their own business and let

you tend to yours—or not?

_____

_____

30. Which one would you rather have work for you—a man that you know well and know to be a good man, or a stranger who is more efficient and faster?

_____

_____

31. If you had to chose between a husband or wife who was a real help around the place or one who was especially warm and loving, which would you prefer? _____

_____

32. When with a group of friends, do you prefer doing such things as singing and visiting with them, or do you prefer to play games where one side wins?

_____

_____

33. Which describes you best?
I work because I need to.

_____

I work because I enjoy it.

_____

34. Here is a set of conditions (on a card) generally regarded as wrong. Which do you consider the very most wrong? _____
next most wrong? _____
next most wrong? _____
next most wrong? _____

next most wrong? _____
the least wrong? _____
A. a woman who is unfaithful to her husband
B. a man who cheats at poker
C. a man who fights with his neighbors
D. a woman who says untrue things in court about others in the community
E. a woman who is sexually available to men and boys in the community
F. a man who is unfaithful to his wife

35. A new way of curing meat has been advertised. You have tasted some cured the new way; some of your friends have used it, and you want to try it on the pork for your family. Your parents think there are dangers in the new chemicals and say so. You think they are safe. Would you go on and cure the meat the new way, or would you do it the way your parents say?

_____

_____

36. Which do you think most people around here would do?

_____

_____

37. Some people think it is important for children to mind their parents just as soon as they are spoken to. Others don't think this is too important. How do you feel?

_____

_____

38. At what age do you think children should make their own decisions?

_____

_____

39. Some folks say: "I'm not interested in hearing a lot of arguments which I don't really agree with." How do you feel about this?

_____

_____

40. Do you think a boy who has completed high school makes a better husband than one who has not?

_____

41. Do you think he makes a better community member?

_____

42. Do you swap out work?

_____

43. With whom do you swap out?

_____

_____

(How did your workgroup get started? Who decides who will be members? Who calls it together? What obligations are involved?)

_____

_____

_____

44. Now I should like to know how you and your (spouse) divide up some of the family jobs.[1]
    A. Who does the shopping?
    B. Who fixes husband's breakfast weekdays?
    C. Who washes up the evening dishes?
    D. Who makes the garden?
    E. Who repairs things around the house?
    F. Who looks after the money and bills?

H-all	H-more than w	w-more than H	w-all
———	———	———	———
———	———	———	———
———	———	———	———
———	———	———	———

45. Among your brothers and sisters who live in this community, if you had a real problem which one do you

1. This instrument was borrowed from John Mogey of Boston University.

think would be the most sympathetic?

_____

46. Which do you think would be the most helpful?

_____

47. Suppose you were buying a tobacco planter that someone had had only a year. How carefully would you feel you had to check its mechanical condition if you were buying from close kin? [2]

_____

if you were buying from a neighbor?

_____

if you were buying from someone in another community?

_____

48. If you had a teenage daughter who needed a ride to Alabama to visit relatives, would you feel right about her taking this all-night drive with her
older brother? _____
uncle? _____
2nd or 3rd cousin? _____
neighbor? _____
a Negro neighbor? _____
a stranger? _____

49. Here is a card with four

lines on it. Think of each line as the way the relatives written by it get along. There are five numbers there, going from free and easy at one end to reserved and distant at the other. There isn't any correct number to circle, but I would like you to give me the number in each case that you think best shows the way these persons in your community usually get along.

husband-wife
father-son
brother-sister
nephew-uncle
    (mother's brother)

free, easy, informal, warm				reserved, distant, stiff, formal
1	2	3	4	5
1	2	3	4	5
1	2	3	4	5
1	2	3	4	5

50. Those who study community life almost always draw a sociogram of the community. A simple sociogram

2. We found this to be a poor question. Valley residents knew what the writer did not know: a tobacco planter is a simple and sturdy machine; very little can "go wrong" with it, especially with a one-year-old planter, which residents interpreted to mean a new machine.

is drawn on this card. The circles stand for persons and the arrows for others who have chosen these persons either as the one they would want most to be with or the one they would want least to be with. In order to make a sociogram we have to have names, but the names will not be told anyone. Actually we are not even interested in names, but we must have them in order to find the positions of the circles in the picture. Would you mind telling me the name that pops in your mind first as I ask these questions?

A. What person do you most prefer working with _____
What person do you least prefer working with? _____

B. What person would you most prefer spending a few free hours with?

_____

What person would you least prefer spending a few free hours with?

_____

C. Name the person you would most likely go to for advice in case of death? _____
Name one you feel you would least likely go to for advice in case of death? _____

D. Who do you think is the most capable of handling community problems?

_____

Who do you think is least capable of handling community problems?

_____

E. Name the three families or individuals you would probably invite to a get-together at your home.
(1) _____
(2) _____
(3) _____

Bibliography

Scientific Works in Sociology and Anthropology

Ackerman, Charles. "Affiliations: Structural Determinants of Differential Divorce Rates," *The American Journal of Sociology*, LXIX, No. 1 (July 1963), 13–20.

Allport, G. W. *Personality, a Psychological Interpretation*. New York: Holt, 1937.

Arensberg, Conrad M., and S. T. Kimball. *Family and Community in Ireland*. Cambridge: Harvard University Press, 1940.

Arensberg, Conrad M., "The Community as Object and as Sample," *American Anthropologist*, LXII, No. 2 (April 1961), 241–264.

Bachofen, J. J. *Das Mutterrecht*. Stuttgart, 1861.

Barnes, J. A. "Marriage and Residential Continuity," *American Anthropologist*, LXII, No. 5 (October 1960), 850–866.

Bates, F. L. "Some Observations Concerning the Structural Aspect of Role Conflict." Paper read before the twenty-fifth annual meeting of the Southern Sociological Association, Louisville, Kentucky, April 1962.

Bennett, John W., and Leo B. Despres. "Kinship and Instrumental Activities: A Theoretical Inquiry," *American Anthropologist*, LXII, No. 2 (April 1960), 254–268.

Berry, Brewton. *Race and Ethnic Relations*. Boston: Houghton Mifflin Co., 1951.

Bogue, Donald J. *The Structure of the Metropolitan Community: A Study of Dominance and Subdominance*. Ann Arbor: University of Michigan Press, 1949.

Bohannan, Paul. *Justice and Judgment Among the Tiv*. London: Oxford University Press, 1957.

———. *Social Anthropology*. New York: Holt, Rinehart & Winston, 1963.

Bott, Elizabeth. *Family and Social Network*. London: Tavistock, 1957.

Brewer, Earl. Unpublished tables from Questions 26–29 of the Southern Appalachian Survey secured through personal communication, 1962.

Broom, Leonard, and Philip Selznick. *Sociology*. New York: Harper & Row, 1963.

160 : *Neighbor and Kin*

Brown, James S. "Social Class, Intermarriage, and Church Membership in a Kentucky Community," *The American Journal of Sociology*, XVII (November 1951), pp. 232–242.

Codere, Helen. "A Genealogical Study of Kinship in the United States," *Psychiatry*, XVIII (1955), 65–80.

Cumming, Elaine, and David M. Schneider. "Sibling Solidarity: A Property of American Kinship," *American Anthropologist*, LXIII, No. 3 (June 1961), 498–508.

Davis, Kingsley. *Human Society*. New York: The Macmillan Co., 1949.

Durkheim, Emile. *The Division of Labor in Society* (1893). Translated by George Simpson. Glencoe, Illinois: The Free Press, 1933.

Eggan, Fred. *Social Anthropology of North American Tribes*. Chicago: The University of Chicago Press, 1955.

Embree, John F. "Thailand, a Loosely Structured System," *American Anthropologist*, LII (April-June 1950), 181–186.

Evans-Pritchard, Edward Evan. *Kinship and Marriage Among the Nuer*. Oxford: Clarendon Press, 1951.

Firth, Raymond. *Two Studies of Kinship in London*. London: The Athlone Press, 1956.

Firth, Raymond, *et al.* "Factions in Indian and Overseas Indian Societies," *British Journal of Sociology*, VIII (1957), 291–342.

Ford, Thomas R. (ed.). *The Southern Appalachian Region, A Survey*. Lexington: University of Kentucky Press, 1962.

Freeman, J. D. "The Iban of Western Borneo" in *Social Structure in Southeast Asia*. Edited by George P. Murdock. Chicago: Quadrangle Books, 1960, pp. 65–88.

Fromm, Erich. *Escape from Freedom*. New York: Rinehart, 1941.

Garigue, Philip. *Études sur le Canada Francais*. Montréal: Université de Montréal, 1958.

Goffman, Erving. *The Presentation of Self in Everyday Life*. Garden City, New York: Doubleday & Co., Inc., 1959.

Hawley, Amos. *Human Ecology*. New York: Ronald Press Co., 1950.

Hillery, G. A. "Definitions of Community: Areas of Agreement," *Rural Sociology*, XX, No. 2 (1955), 111–123.

Homans, George. *The Human Group*. New York: Harcourt, Brace, 1950.

Hughes, Everett C. *French Canada in Transition*. Chicago: University of Chicago Press, 1943.

Hunter, Floyd. *Community Power Structure*. Chapel Hill: University of North Carolina Press, 1953.

Katz, Alvin, and Reuben Hill. "Residential Propinquity and Marital Selection: A Review of Theory, Method, and Fact," *Marriage and Family Living*, XX (1958), 27–35.

Keesing, F. M. *Cultural Anthropology*. New York: Rinehart Co., 1958.

Kerckhoff, Alan C. "Some Contributions to the Social Systems Analysis of the Family." Paper read before the twenty-fifth annual meeting of the Southern Sociological Association, Louisville, Kentucky, April, 1962.

Kerr, Madeline. *Personality and Conflict in Jamaica.* Liverpool: University Press, 1952.

Krige, J. D. "The Social Function of Witchcraft," *Theoria: A Journal of Studies of the Arts Faculty, Natal University College,* I (1947), 8–21.

Kroeber, A. L. "Classificatory Systems of Relationship," *The Journal of the Royal Anthropological Institute of Great Britain and Ireland,* XXXIX (1909), 77–85.

———. *Anthropology.* New York: Harcourt, Brace, 1948.

Leach, E. R. "The Sinhalese of the Dry Zone of Northern Ceylon" in *Social Structure in Southeast Asia.* Edited by George P. Murdock. Chicago: Quadrangle Books, 1960, pp. 116–127.

Lévi-Strauss, Claude. *Anthropologie Structurale.* Paris: Plon, 1958.

Linton, Ralph. *The Study of Man.* New York: D. Appleton-Century, 1936.

Lockwood, David. "Some Remarks on 'The Social System,'" *British Journal of Sociology,* VII (June 1956), 134–146.

Loomis, Charles P., and J. A. Beegle. *Rural Social Systems.* New York: Prentice-Hall, Inc., 1950.

Lowie, Robert Harry. *The Crow Indians.* New York: Farrar & Rinehart, 1935.

M'Lennan, John F. *Primitive Marriage.* Edinburgh: Adam & Charles Black, 1865.

Maine, Sir Henry. *Ancient Law.* London: Murray, 1861.

Malinowski, Bronislaw. *The Family Among the Australian Aborigines.* London: University of London Press, 1913.

Merton, Robert K. *Social Theory and Social Structure.* Glencoe, Illinois: The Free Press, 1957.

Millar, John. *The Observations Concerning the Distinction of Ranks in Society.* Glasgow, 1771.

Miner, Horace M. *St. Denis, A French Canadian Parish.* Chicago: University of Chicago Press, 1939.

Mogey, John. *Rural Life in Northern Ireland.* London: Oxford University Press, 1947.

———. *Family and Neighbourhood.* Oxford: University Press, 1956.

———. "The Climate of Opinion on Housing Estates," *The Sociological Review,* IV, No. 1 (July 1956), Keele, Staffordshire: The University College of North Staffordshire, 63–76.

———. "Introduction," *International Journal of Comparative Sociology,* III, No. 2 (September 1962).

Moore, Wilbert E. "Three Views of the Businessman," *Duns' Review and Modern Industry,* LXXX, No. 6 (December 1962), 31, 63–66.

Morgan, Lewis H. *Systems of Consanguinity and Affinity of the Human Family.* Washington: Smithsonian Institution, 1870.

Morton, Frederic. *The Rothschilds.* New York: Atheneum, 1961.

Murdock, George P. *Social Structure.* New York: Macmillan, 1949.

Nadel, S. F. *The Theory of Social Structure*. London: Cohen & West, 1957.

Norbeck, Edward. *Religion in Primitive Society*. New York: Harper, 1961.

Parsons, Talcott. *The Social System*. Glencoe, Illinois: The Free Press, 1951.

————. "An Outline of the Social System" in *Theories of Society*, Vol. I. Edited by Talcott Parsons, *et al.* New York: The Free Press of Glencoe, Inc., 1961.

Pehrson, Robert N. "Bilateral Kin Groupings as a Structural Type," *Journal of East Asiatic Studies*, III, No. 2 (January 1954), 199–203.

Piddington, Ralph. "A Study of French Canadian Kinship," *International Journal of Comparative Sociology*, II, No. 1 (March 1961), 3–23.

Polsky, Ned. "The Village Beat Scene: Summer, 1960," *Dissent*, VIII, No. 3 (1961), 339–359.

Radcliffe-Brown, A. R. *Structure and Function in Primitive Society*. London: Cohen & West, 1952.

Radcliffe-Brown, A. R., and Daryl Forde. *African Systems of Kinship and Marriage*. Oxford: Oxford University Press, 1956.

Redfield, Robert. *The Primitive World and Its Transformations*. Ithaca, New York: Cornell University Press, 1953.

————. *The Little Community: Viewpoints for the Study of a Human Whole*. Chicago: University of Chicago Press, 1955.

Rivers, W. H. R. *The Todas*. New York: Macmillan, 1906.

Robinson, W. S. "The Logical Structure of Analytic Induction," *American Sociological Review*, XVI (December 1951), 812–818.

Rodman, Hyman. "The Lower-Class Value Stretch," *Social Forces*, XLII, No. 2 (December 1963), 205–216.

Saal, C. D. "Causes of the Delay in Western European Family Research and Some Notes of the Investigations of the Dutch Rural Family" in *Studies of the Family*, Vol. I. Edited by Nels Anderson. Goettingen: Vandenhoeck & Ruprecht, 1954, 229–245.

Schneider, David, and George Homans. "Kinship Terminology and the American Kinship System," *American Anthropologist*, LVII (1955), 1194–1208.

Sherman, Mandel, and Thomas R. Henry. *Hollow Folk*. New York: Thomas Y. Crowell Co., 1933.

Siegel, Bernard, and Alan R. Beals. "Pervasive Factionalism," *American Anthropologist*, LXII, No. 3 (June 1960), 394–417.

Simmel, Georg. *Conflict*. Translated by Kurt H. Wolff. Glencoe, Illinois: The Free Press, 1955.

Sprott, W. J. H. "Principia Sociologica," *The British Journal of Sociology*, III, No. 3 (September 1952), 203–221.

Stouffer, Samuel A. "Intervening Opportunities: A Theory Relating Mobility and Distance," *American Sociological Review*, V (December 1940), 845–867.

Sussman, Marvin B., and Lee Burchinal. "Kin Family Network: Unheralded Structure in Current Conceptualizations of Family Functioning." *Marriage and Family Living*, XXIV, No. 3 (1962), 231–240.

Vogt, Evon Z. *Modern Homesteaders*. Cambridge: The Belknap Press, 1955.

Warner, W. Lloyd, and P. S. Lunt. *The Social Life of a Modern Community*. New Haven: Yale University Press, 1941.

Warner, W. Lloyd, and Associates. *Democracy in Jonesville: A Study of Quality and Inequality*. New York: Harper, 1949.

Weber, Max. *The Theory of Social and Economic Organization*. Translated by A. M. Henderson and Talcott Parsons and edited by Talcott Parsons. Glencoe, Illinois: The Free Press, 1947.

———. *Protestant Ethic and the Spirit of Capitalism*. Translated by Talcott Parsons. New York: Charles Scribner's Sons, 1956.

Whiting, B. B. *Paiute Sorcery*. New York: Viking Fund Publications in Anthropology, No. 15, 1950.

Willems, Emilio. *Antropologia Social*. Sao Paulo: Difusao Européia do Livro, 1962.

Wilson, Monica Hunter. "Witch Beliefs and Social Structure," *The American Journal of Sociology*, Vol. LVI, No. 4 (January 1951), 307–313.

Wissler, Clark. *Indians of the United States*. New York: Doubleday, Doran & Co., 1940.

Wolf, Eric R. "Closed Corporate Peasant Communities in Mesoamerica and Central Java," *Southwestern Journal of Anthropology*, Vol. XIII (1957), 1–19.

Young, Michael, and Peter Willmott. *Family and Kinship in East London*. London: Routledge & Kegan Paul, 1957.

Zimmerman, Carle Clark. *Family and Civilization*. New York: Harper, 1947.

Federal Records

U. S. Bureau of the Census. Mach. # 101. Photographed in Microfilm Lab.
    7th Census, 1850, Tennessee.
    8th Census, 1860, Tennessee.
    9th Census, 1870, Tennessee.
    10th Census, 1880, Tennessee.

U. S. Bureau of the Census. *Statistical Abstract of the United States, 1963*. 84th Annual Edition. Washington, D. C., 1963.

U. S. Department of Justice, Federal Bureau of Investigation. *Uniform Crime Reports for the United States*. Vol. XXVII, No. 2, 1956.

Kinbrace County Data

Note: The reader will keep in mind that the remainder of this bibliography makes use of a fictitious county name.

Kinbrace County History

Goodspeed Publishing Co. *History of Tennessee*. Nashville: The Goodspeed Publishing Co., 1886.

Hale, Will T., and Dixon L. Merritt. *A History of Tennessee and Tennesseans*, Vol. VIII. Chicago: The Lewis Publishing Co., 1913.

Vertical Files on Kinbrace County History, Tennessee State Library and Archives, Nashville.

Kinbrace County Maps

General Highway Map, Kinbrace County, Tennessee, 1951. Tennessee State Highway Department.

Kinbrace County Rural Delivery Routes, February 25, 1914.

Kinbrace County, 1937. Department of Conservation, Tennessee State Geological Department, Nashville, Tennessee.

Map of Kinbrace County, 1878. (By districts, with farms and businesses named.)

Kinbrace County Newspapers

Advocate—Extra, Saturday Morning, April 11, 1814.

The Gazette, 1822–1823.

Western Weekly Review, 1831–1867.

The Weekly Review, 1867–1875.

Kinbrace County News, 1875–1962.

Kinbrace County Records

Circuit Court Records and Grand Jury Records. Circuit Court Clerk's Office.

Will Record Books, 1819–1858.

Tennessee Records of Kinbrace County. Copied Under Work's Progress Administration, 1937.

    Bible, Family, Marriage, and Tombstone Records.

    County Court Minute Books, 1800–1815.

    Wills and Inventories, 1800–1830.

Index

Ackerman, Charles, 123

Adaptations: involving "outside" world, 72–73; as control mechanism, 133 and *n*, 134; and status equalization, 139; and the explanation of strain, 139–143 *passim*

Affective-instrumental dimension: in a particularistic-ascriptive structure, xxx, xxxi; in kinship relations, 33–35, 128 and *n*, 129, 131; and the validity problem, 151

Age at marriage: early, ideal for female, 11, 12; gap between spouses, 12

Aged, the. *See* Old people

Agricultural tools, circulated through auctions, 19

Allport, G. W., 139

Ambition: regarded with disapproval, 75, 77, 136, 142–143; lack of, in ascribed system, 133

Anglo-Saxon sibship, identical kin status within, 11

Animals, subject of country-store talk, 49

Applecross, naming of, 4–5

Applecross-Millstone: spatial aspects, 45, 46; collateral ties in, 46, 48, 53, 141, 142; work in relation to community boundaries, 46, 47, 48, 53; residence patterns, 46, 53, 54; size of farms, 47; absentee landowner in, 47–

48; use of country store, 48, 53; church attendance, 51, 53; lack of formal organizations, 51, 53; school attendance, 51, 53; education and ambition, 53, 54; material possessions, 54; lack of status differentiation, 54; segregated marital roles in, 61–62, 63, 65; farming activities, 61–67; swapping out practice, 63–67; reciprocity in, 64; neighbor relations as economic arrangements in, 63, 67; absence of "outside" contacts, 73; feelings against status-related factors, 74–78 *passim*; lack of leadership seen in sociometric choices, 78–79; control mechanisms in, 133, 134; integration within, 137; open-family, closed-community structure, 139–143 *passim*; explanation of harmony in, 142. *See also* Lower Ridge area

Applecross Store, early tavern, 4

Arensberg, Conrad M., xxvi, ix

Auctioneer: role of, 16–17, 18*n*; characteristics of, 17, 18–19; as scapegoat, 104

Auctions: used for property transference, 14–20 *passim*; and runaway marriage system, 15; community control through, 16; county seat, 17, 18; features of, 18–19; functions of, 19–20; as scapegoat device, 19; tobacco,

Multiple kinship ties, affecting tense relations, 102–103

Multiple marriage: patterns in genealogies, 8–9, 23, 38–40; and the strong collateral bond, 10–11, 22, 35, 36; between cousins and siblings, 22, 35–37; and divorce, 40; and union between young man and old woman, 40; and relation to deceased spouse's sibling, 123. *See also* Close kin marriage, Cousin marriage

Murder: "cold-blooded," defined, 88; accounts from county newspapers, 96–100 *passim;* relation of slayer to slain, 99, 100; examples of Ridge, 108–109; not followed by reprisal, 112; no one willing to file suit or testify, 112 and *n. See also* Violence

Murdock, George P., xxvi, 10*n*, 112, 120

Muskogian tribes, 94–95

Naming patterns: collateral ties reflected in, 27; multiple names for each relative, 30–31. *See also* Given names; Nicknames; Surnames

Nashville, Tennessee, xxvi, 25, 50*n*, 59, 89

Negroes: building of old homestead, 7; and "Uncle" and "Aunt" titles, 32; in country store talk, 50; use of old schoolhouse, 52; mystic powers of Negro church, 52, 104–105; woman with occult gifts, 104; hanging, 105; "Free Julie," 105; jokes about, 111

Neighbors: and economic arrangements in Applecross-Millstone, 67; relations with, identified with swapping out, 67; keeping up with business of, 67; importance of getting along with, 67, 90, 92–93; *vs.* kin, which to expect most from, 90; *vs.* friend,

in a rural system, 90; *vs.* friend, and ascription *vs.* achievement, 90; *vs.* kin, feelings toward children of, 91; invited to home for social gathering, 92; in cases of joking and homicide, 100; kin and community relations secondary to, 112*n. See also* Fighting with neighbors

Nephews, 102

Nephew-uncle, tense relations between, 100–103 *passim*

Newspapers, county, used in study of violence, 96–99

Nicknames: humorous, 29–30; and abbreviated names, 29–30; signify "belonging," 30; multiple, 30–31; surname, function of, 30 and *n*

Nieces, 102

Nonsuccess ideology: applied to Ridge community norms, 78, 136; and the explanation of strain, 142–143. *See also* Egalitarian norms; So-So; Status; Success

Norbeck, Edward, 103*n*, 105

Old people: stories about, 5–6; described, 6; respect for wishes of, 32; feelings against hard work of, 77

"Outsiders." *See* External relations

Owls, 104

Parent-child relation, instrumental nature of, 33, 34

Parsons, Talcott, xiv, xxx–xxxii, 73, 74, 125–133 *passim*

Particularism *vs.* universalism: in a particularistic-ascriptive structure, xxx; in punishing gasoline thieves, 90–91

Particularistic-achievement structure, xxxi*n*, 130–131

Particularistic-ascriptive structure: characteristics of, xxx, xxxi–xxxii, 125, 129–132; and lack of external relations, 73; lack of

So-So (*Cont.*)
misunderstood in modern democracy, 145; values, respect for, 146
Spatial aspects of Ridge community, 45–46
Speed in work: attitudes against, 66, 67, 77; boy and mule criticized for, 77
Sprott, W. J. H., xxxii, 138
Squire, 11
Status: ascriptive cues preferred in particularistic-ascriptive structure, xxx, xxxi, 125; minimum distinction in male and female naming patterns, 28–29; differentiation in Turnabout Hollow, 54; distinctions minimum in Applecross-Millstone, 74–78, 134, 135; emblems, disapproved, 75, 136, 142–143; ascribed, and "Miss Abbie" ideal, 79; emphasis on neighbor rather than friend, 90; pattern-maintenance based on ascribed, 133, 134; equalization, function of social substructures, 136–137; symbols, escape from, 145; equalizing processes at work in American society, 145. *See also* Egalitarian norms; Nonsuccess ideology; So-So; Stratification
Stills: as closed family operations, 67, 68; requirements for, 68–69; convictions for operating, 96, 97, 98
Stories, told to protect stills, 68–69, 70
Strain, evidences of, 103. *See* Tension
Strangers: marrying, 14, 51, 55, 109; "rank stranger" defined, 17; at local auctions, 17–18; eliminated in swapping out, 66; norms against hiring, 66, 67; and friends *vs.* kin status, 89*n;* and violence, 109
Stratification: absent, implications for basic theory of, xii–xiv, xxiii,

140; and violence, above and below Ridge, 113; adaptation without, 133, 134. *See also* Egalitarian norms; Nonsuccess ideology; So-So; Status
Stripping tobacco, 63, 65
Study of Tennessee Ridge community: three contributions to sociology, vii–xiv *passim;* goals, xxvii–xxviii, xxix; plan of book, xxix; using sociology and anthropology, xxix, 151; focused on solving two problems, xxix; approach used in explaining social structure, xxix; theoretical insight considered most significant, 124; two surprises of, 134–135; sources of data, 149, 151; gaining access to community, 149; interviewing and visiting, 149–150; informants, 150; reliability checks, 150–151; validity problems and aids, 151
Stumps, haunted, significance in still operations, 105
Styles, women's, 87
Success: as defined in area of study, xii; ideology, and the "Go-Go" culture, 144, 145; evidences of escape from, 145; beyond one's aspirations, 145. *See also* Nonsuccess ideology
Suicide: of college girl, 57, accounts from county newspapers, 96, 97, 98; following land or love loss, 110
Supernatural power, persons with, as sign of strain, 103
Superstition, and protection of stills, 69
Surnames: keeping farms in the same, 13, 14–15; keeping same, in marriages, 23, 26; identical with given names, 29; use of nicknames for, 30; and forms of address, 31
Surplus. *See* Excess